I0437085

Amid the
Shadows

A Paranormal Point of View

Amid the Shadows

A Paranormal Point of View

Gary Price

Copyright © 2012 by Gary Price.

Library of Congress Control Number:		2012921369
ISBN:	Hardcover	978-1-4797-4909-6
	Softcover	978-1-4797-4908-9
	Ebook	978-1-4797-4910-2

All rights reserved. No part of this book may be reproduced or transmitted in any form or by any means, electronic or mechanical, including photocopying, recording, or by any information storage and retrieval system, without permission in writing from the copyright owner.

This book was printed in the United States of America.

To order additional copies of this book, contact:
Xlibris Corporation
1-888-795-4274
www.Xlibris.com
Orders@Xlibris.com
124689

DEDICATION

I dedicate this, my first written words, to my love and my life, Anna Price, who has supported me throughout all that I endeavor. For my wife—with her, I conquer all!

PREFACE

S THE TITLE of this book states, "amid the shadows," I feel that while standing in the darkness and the unknown during my search for answers, I am among others not of this world! There are so many untold stories, so many hidden secrets within the walls, pathways, and the very essence of that in which we so desperately search. Being a paranormal investigator, I deal with the many unexplainable aspects within the spiritual realm on a daily basis. I write my thoughts down and share them with others in the paranormal community. This has been a learning experience, both for me and for others who read and share their experiences with me. This book is a compilation of different beliefs and thoughts I have concerning the paranormal realm and the many dark and enlightening experiences I have encountered. As you turn the pages of this book, try to put yourself in my shoes and follow in my footsteps with an open mind. You will find many deep and mind-provoking subjects that will make you stop for a minute and reflect on how you have viewed the paranormal in the past, how you view it currently, and how you may change your outlook and approach in the future. The untold stories are out there, and the answers are out there, so when you are amid the shadows, stop and listen to the stories that are about to befall you!

There are two major mistakes we can make in our lives as we travel the road to finding truth and reason to events that occur in a spiritual realm. One is not continuing the journey to the very end while enduring and conquering all obstacles before us. The other is not starting this wondrous and mysterious journey at all, not taking that very vital first step. Begin your journey and stay the path and follow your passion!

This book is dedicated to all of you that share the same passion that I hold dear for the paranormal. We all must do it for the right reasons, not for the thrill of the moment, not for the popularity it could bring, and not for the bragging rights. We do it for one reason and one reason alone—to find the answers others fear. With me, it is my passion, and I make it my journey to understand and do it with compassion. So I ask you to join me on this trek as we walk together amid the shadows!

Encounter No. 1:
The Journey Begins

NO MATTER THE forum, the question always arises: "Gary, what first piqued your interest into the paranormal?" In response, I would have to say it started at a very young age. I was seven years old at the time and living in a small town called Cambridge, which is located in Ohio. It was a quiet and peaceful town where everybody pretty much kept to themselves. The house I lived in at the time looked to be of a Victorian style, a majestic off-green three-story structure.

When evening arrived and I was sent off to bed, strange things would begin to occur, which would forever change my view of the paranormal. As I lay bundled in my bed, I would hear strange noises as if someone were dragging their dry and scratchy feet across the worn and creaky hardwood floors that were part of my room. I would never see anything but always thought it to be strange and, at that age, figured it a good idea to wrap up tightly and cover my head. This became almost a nightly occurrence, and being the age I was, it was scaring me to the point where I needed to tell my parents. But my fears fell upon deaf ears as they would write it off as the age of the home or an active child's imagination, basically the same thing most of us do today. As this event continued to occur day in and day out, it began to progress to the point of utter terror as now a human form materialized before my very eyes. While I ignored the sounds in the night as my parents thought would help, something thought it necessary to materialize and initiate contact with me. Physical touch had now become an eerie part of this nightmare I would experience. As I gathered what courage a seven-year-old child could draw from himself, I would look into the face of darkness, and it did chill me to my very soul. The apparition of a child about the same age as I am now stood beside my bed as if staring right through me. I could barely make out the legs, but he wore a white shirt, and his face was most distinguishable—at least what was there! He had shining black hair, which was as dark as night, but still it seemed to emit an aura of light. As I remember, the ears were visible, but the face horrified me most. There were absolutely no facial features—no eyes, no nose, no mouth, only a gleaming flesh that moved about as if trying to speak but could not. In holy terror, I ran from my room, screaming all the way down the hall to my parents' room, again met with the explanation of a youthful imagination.

What else could I do but relive this horror night after night? The bed I had at the time was an older-style bunk bed, and the bottom portion had now become my fortress as I would tuck blankets and sheets around its exterior to create a shelter much like a tent. At my age, this seemed like a great idea to stop the interactions I was experiencing. No such luck; whatever it was that chose to visit me throughout each night had the strength and the ability to strike at the covers and at times pull them away. Knowing no one would believe me, I had no choice but to deal with this in my own way. I would watch the apparition more adamantly as it moved about my room, as if floating effortlessly. The point soon arrived when it began to move toward my bedroom window and surprisingly seemed to fade right through it. This continued for a few nights until finally I conjured up the courage to move toward the window and see where this entity might have been going. Looking out from my third-floor window, I was about to see the most eerie and frightening thing that still to this day sends terrifying chills up my spine. As I stared down toward the backyard, now illuminated by bits of moonlight, I saw this apparition of darkness crouched next to an old well, which at the time was covered and sealed by a permanent concrete block. With his neck twisted in an unnatural way, his faceless head glared up at me and beckoned for me to follow, to come to him in the night. Then suddenly, in a jerking and ominous fashion much like you see imitated in the horror films of today, he crawled on all fours into the structure as if being consumed by it.

At this point, I became violently ill and ran into the bathroom. I can still remember the icy cold that I felt and the numbness that had now taken over my body. I awoke the next morning lying on the bathroom floor and immediately notified my parents. And as any other parent would do, they primarily wrote it off once again and even showed a bit of dissatisfaction toward my repeated efforts to convince them. As you can imagine, I sat up the following nights awaiting my visitor from another realm as I would stare deep into an emptiness and in horrified anticipation of his return. But from that night on, I was never witness to this visit from the shadows again. We eventually moved from the home, and I grew and moved on to start my own life. I still wonder to this very day about what happened those many years ago. Was this child somehow trying to tell me he drowned in this well? Or was he perhaps murdered and hidden away within its dark, damp, cold, and embracing walls? I will never know, but I can tell you this one thing for certain—that this experience and many others long after that have motivated me and ignited a passion deep within me to research the paranormal and try to make sense of an afterlife and the things that occur within another realm.

ENCOUNTER NO. 2: HAUNTED SPAIN

AFTER GROWING UP and moving away to begin my life, I found myself stationed in Spain as a military member with the United States Air Force. While there, I lived in base housing, which at the time was approximately twenty miles from the base itself. The homes themselves were duplexes but one on top of the other and were quite old. I believe the military had acquired them at a fair price from the Spanish government. The area was beautiful as it was located away from the hustle and bustle of everyday life and set more in a small countryside community. Little did I know that one day I was to experience an even more horrifying encounter with something I believe to this very day was of a malevolent and malicious nature.

My life in this new environment was difficult for a while as I was not acclimated with the new ways and surroundings until quite a while had passed. As I began to settle in and became comfortable with this new venture in my life, I began to take some time and updated my home to where I felt more at ease. This didn't involve any major construction but only minor add-ons basically aimed at a beautification process. It was at this time that strange occurrences began in the home. I can remember specifically one event that still perplexes me every time I think back on it. After hitting the hay for some long-needed slumber one night, I heard what sounded like someone tapping at my front door. I arose and stepped out to my living area to see what it might be. Keep in mind that living so far from the base itself, I was constantly standing vigil because of some local factions who would rather not have us there. While pulling back the curtain that was next to my door, I did not notice anything whatsoever outside. Then the tapping could be heard once again. But this time I knew where it was coming from. It was from the new macramé hanging table I had just installed the very same morning. There was a slight movement as I could make out a light swaying from where I stood. I had no pets, and there were no vents in this type of structure, so I found this to be quite odd. As I approached the table to try and make sense of this occurrence, I was met halfway with what felt like two ice-cold hands gripping me just above each knee. I froze in my tracks and then jumped back and hit the light switch. There was nothing there, absolutely nothing, only the table continuing to sway and the now-crumpled rug in the center of the room. I had nothing between myself and the table but space. So what was it that grabbed me at knee level? I was soon to find out.

About one week later, I had arrived home after a long military exercise and was ready for a long-awaited, peaceful, solemn night's rest. All I had planned to do that evening before retiring was hang a new cabinet in my bathroom. Blowing off the previous experience that I had to some sort of muscle spasm, I continued and finished my little project in no time at all. I then showered and prepared for bed, and as I exited the shower, I could see that the new cabinet door was open. Okay, maybe I forgot to shut it, so I closed it. Leaving the bathroom, I heard the audible click of the latching system on the cabinet once again, so I returned to check it out. Lo and behold, there was the door wide open again. I thought to myself, what the hell, did I get a defective cabinet and need to go exchange it? I closed it once more and stood there for at least a minute this time. Nothing happened, so I turned to walk away, and guess what occurred. Nope, the cabinet did not open again, but this time, the harsh slap of what felt like two hands on the upper portion of my back legs. This really freaked me out a bit and caused me to think back to the time I was seven and the events that had taken place then. Was it happening to me again but with some other force from the other side? Unknowingly, my answer was to come to me that very night!

I lay down my head, and it wasn't long before I was off to dreamland. Then it began at two o'clock, a night that I will never forget and that will haunt me deep to my very soul. I heard a noise once again in the pitch of night, only this time it was of a scratching nature, much like tiny claws. Still spooked from my previous experience, I reached beside my bed and picked up the baseball bat I kept for protection. I thought to myself, "This may be a rat that found its way in somehow." And believe me when I say that they were quite large in this country. As I headed down the hallway, which led from my bedroom, I heard the scratching getting louder as I approached the bathroom. The floors were ice cold and were made of concrete as were the walls on each side of me, which was a very confined area to move through. It was pitch-dark, and the only light source was from the moonlight creeping in from the living room area. I now stood directly in front of the bathroom door, which was ajar only a bit. The scratching, now more pronounced, came from the back side of the door itself, so I slowly reached out for the handle. As I began to push the door inward, the scratching stopped, and I began to think that, yes, there must be some sort of animal that found its way in. Tightly gripping the bat, I pushed the door to fully open and, with the other hand, began to reach for the light switch. But before I made it to the switch, something hideous and terrifying threw me backward into the concrete hallway wall. I am not sure if it was a reflex or an actual force, but there I was, back against the wall, staring in horror as this terrifying event unfolded before my very eyes! Out of the bathroom came flying a tiny girl, hair glowing, blonde, and maybe about the age of eight. The eeriest part of this was, she had the blackest eyes I had ever seen. She donned an illuminating white dress with a bright red ribbon around the waist. She was running, and the shrill was heard of her voice, which echoed a horrifying scream, evil laughing and sorrowful crying all at the same time. Her arms were outstretched toward the floor as if chasing something and trying to retrieve it, and I could hear the trample of little feet as if they were wearing some type of hard-soled shoes. She moved like the wind down the hallway away from me and faded at the end. My heart at this time was pounding uncontrollably, and I immediately arose to give chase. But nothing remained to be seen even after I turned on every light in the home—nothing. I stayed up the rest of that night and carried on the next day. I would not share this story with anyone as I knew I would look quite loony in the process. To make sense of this has perplexed me for many years. It never reoccurred after that day, and I spent the rest of my time there with no activity at all. This one event in itself drove me to begin my research into the paranormal, which I continue to do so to this day.

Encounter No. 3:
It's Not A Game Anymore

FTER MEETING MY commitment to the military, it was once again time to move on. I figured at this time I could commit myself fully to trying to find answers to events that tend to occur in a spiritual or paranormal realm. I was ready to build my own paranormal research group. I wanted a group of people with diverse and individual beliefs, religions, views, and values. The only question remaining at this point was, was I really ready myself? I was soon to find out that although the passion and mind-set were there, I still would not be prepared for what was soon to come!

Thinking back on my past experiences, I was driven to find out answers, any sort of explanation as to why these things had occurred in my life. My passion to learn more at this point became an obsession, which, while overwhelming at times, was to soon lead to the most horrifying learning experience I had ever encountered in my life.

There I was, all set to go. I had my paranormal team, an arsenal of investigative equipment at my fingertips, and the ways and means to gain access into one of the most haunted locations in Utah. The old, abandoned Tooele Hospital located in Tooele, Utah, was now my primary target. There were many stories about this old structure that intrigued me so much that I would do anything to get in there. The opportunity had finally arrived, and after contacting the owners of the building, I was given permission to bring in my team and conduct an overnight investigation. We were to be locked in for the entire night, and we were passionate about collecting evidence of the spirits that inhabited this majestic structure. I was bound and determined to make contact with those that had been trapped in a spiritual realm within the walls of this sorrow-filled place.

I had visited the hospital on a previous occasion where we were given a tour of the complex by another paranormal group. Though it was short-lived and many others attended, I was witness to what I determined to be a full-body apparition during the tour. As we stood in this eerie pitch-black place, off in a room once occupied by patients long ago, I see it out of the corner of my eye. It was a nurse donned in full medical garb as she passed in front of the door. I thought to myself, "Wait, this anomaly is generating its own light source. I shouldn't be seeing this!" As I rushed out of the room and tried to follow this apparition, I saw it arrive at the old nurses' station connected to the hallway leading to many patient rooms. Then to my surprise, the image faded into the darkness as if it were a dissipating mist caught up in a vortex of cleansing wind. It was at that point the hook was set, the bait had been taken, and my obsession for returning here would be a driving force that would become an obsession for months to follow.

So the long awaited day finally came. My team and I arrived, and we were very excited to finally try and put reason to the events that had occurred previously. We began to set up our equipment, and after approximately two hours, we were ready to go. The night ahead would soon prove to be the most horrifying and life-changing experience that I was ever to bear witness! We proceeded with our normal protocol, which involved starting with EVP (electronic voice phenomenon) sessions throughout the different areas of the hospital. As we moved along, we determined it was time to split off into smaller groups and cover more territory. My focus at this point was to move to the room said to have been inhabited by an evil and malevolent spirit as determined by psychics and mediums who had visited previously. Entering the old and decrepit room at first sent chills up and down my spine as every hair on my body stood on end. Was this due to a presence in the room or just my own excitement and electrified passion? The answer to this question was soon to come!

With one other investigator at my side, we began our EVP session in this room. Being fairly new at investigating, I launched my verbal attack. Provocation at the time seemed to be a great idea as I thought it would stir up the type of activity I was seeking. I called out to the spirit in the room; I shouted obscenities and threatened it with physical harm as I continued to belittle it. This was not like me, I thought to myself, but I was bound and determined to draw out the entity said to be an occupant here. After continuous provocation, we sat in silence for some time without any reaction to my harsh and attacking words. This irritated me more than ever, and being the desperate idiot that I was at the time, I developed a strategic and dangerous tactic I was willing to attempt. Out of desperate arrogance, I called out to this so-called evil spirit. I laid myself on the floor directly in the place it had been previously known to have attempted possession and physical contact with others. I dared it to attack me. I invited it to enter my own body just to experience and prove to myself that these things do exist. Looking back on this, I know it was total stupidity, and I was soon to find out just how stupid of a mistake it really was!

After no results were achieved, we moved forward with our investigation and covered every inch of the building. We would encounter many events and occurrences during this night as we would discover in our evidence later: pictures of what seemed to be shadows staring at us through the dark hallways, peeking from the rooms they once occupied, and the noises of objects being thrown and the voice of a child as he interacted with us, which was to become our most clear and spine-chilling EVP capture to date. But the most horrifying and concrete piece of evidence ever captured in my lifetime was one I was to regret more than anything.

After returning home and conducting review of all video and audio collected from the hospital over the next few days, I was quite impressed with our results. But what was about to transpire would change my views and beliefs permanently. While lying in bed one night, I was awakened by a loud thump much like a fist hitting against the wall. I jumped up and looked around the room but saw nothing, then it happened. Bright green lights that resembled the laser grid I utilized during my investigations appeared across the ceiling. I am talking about thousands of beams of light as they moved across the ceiling toward the bedroom door. Now my laser grid was kept away in a case in a totally different room than my bedroom at the time. I did not know what to think and primarily wrote it off as my eyes attempted to focus after being startled from a deep sleep. This was only the beginning of the dark things that were to come. The following night, I was again awakened by a disturbing noise. Only this time, as I looked up from my pillow, standing there beside me was an image of a small girl in a hospital gown. She just stood there, staring toward me. Her hair was long, stringy, and black in color. Her arms hung to her sides with no movement whatsoever. I rubbed my eyes in disbelief only to still see her remain there before me, but now she swayed from side to side for about ten or more seconds and then faded into nothing. Again, I could not believe my eyes. The next morning, at exactly 6:45 am, I woke to the metal handles of my dresser banging against the wooden drawers. At first I thought the dog might be nosing around and bumping against them; that was not to be the case. As I looked over, I could see the handle physically raise and then drop rapidly. I thought, "No way did that just happen!" And as I stared longer, the movement started on the two drawers directly above, left handle on one, right handle on the other. I rose quickly and went to the dresser, and the activity ceased. I kept this to myself only because there was no way to explain it logically and, at the same time, I did not want to spook others in the house.

Over the next few weeks, my wife would experience voices of females and males, both in bed and during daylight hours around the house. This never occurred with me, but with everything else I had seen, I did not dismiss her concerns. While sitting in the dining room and working on a project, I heard my wife's startled voice. This time, she had been slapped across the leg, and now I was beginning to worry as it seemed that whatever was there was using my family as playthings, knowing that it would disturb me considerably. The same night, as we sat on the couch enjoying a TV show, my wife felt a sharp, burning sensation across the calf of her left leg. At first we thought maybe an ant had found its way in and bitten her as they had done in the past. As she lifted her leg, I noticed three very large welts begin to appear, and they were quite substantial. That was all I needed; it was time to do something about this.

Realizing that through my own stupidity I had brought a malevolent attachment into my own home and that now it was choosing to attack someone dear to me was all I needed. It was time to do something about it. In desperation, I contacted someone educated in the art of cleansing a home of such attachments. I never put much worth into this cleansing process until it was a last resort for the safety of my own family. The cleansing ritual complete, we have experienced no activity whatsoever in our home since. But I have learned so much from just this one experience to never again show such arrogant disrespect or use provocation for such a selfish reason. In the writings that are about to follow, you will see how I have changed and what my own views on the paranormal realm have developed and grown into as we begin to see my apparitions of thought as they appear to me amid the shadows.

CAREFUL, YOU MAY FIND IT!

SOME OF US search throughout to find any proof of a paranormal existence. We crawl into the darkest of places and the thickest of shadows and pry ourselves into every nook and cranny to see if something dark and evil may be lying in wait. Of course, we would rather make contact with a soul or spirit of good nature and light. But what about the evil and demonic possibilities we may eventually face? In life, some people will blame all the bad and undesirable things that occur in their lives on the demons they face day to day. Then there are those who choose to exist in an ignorant bliss of a spiritual war that rages around them. But there are actually some out there within the paranormal field who consider searching for demons to be a great hunt. The game to be bagged and mounted on the wall as the object of their conquering achievement. By doing so, do you think that they allow unfettered access to our sphere of influence to this physical world? Evil is out there, and I constantly stress that we remain vigil in our processes as paranormal investigators. Demons roam in our realm and want nothing more than to pull us into the abyss of emptiness and suffering they have been sentenced to spend eternity in. During this time of year, the sensationalism of dark spirits is magnified tenfold because of Halloween and the eeriness that accompanies it. The common portrayal of Satan as a red-faced man with horns, tail, and pitchfork stands in stark contrast to what really lies in wait for an unsuspecting soul. We need not taunt those in the night who possess malicious intention. We need not open a portal or ourselves up to their malevolent ways. So as we search throughout the realm, remain vigil, for there is a formidable enemy lying in wait. The enemies in the spiritual realm are real, and they are out to devour our very souls and seek to destroy lives and good. A call to arms, you might say. Be careful out there. You may find what you're looking for!

MY MORALITY

T HE IDEA OF morals and values is one of the most relative topics in the world of paranormal investigative practices. Lifetimes can be spent philosophizing about the morality of our human race and the shared "innate" values that exist within it. But what it all boils down to in the end is how we conduct ourselves while we attempt communication with those that have passed, as well as those who still live. There is a code of values that guides the human race toward certain choices and actions, and it is these exact choices and actions that determine the purpose and the course we will eventually take to achieve success. We must choose our actions, values, and goals by the standard of that which is compassionate to others to include souls that have since passed. So consider not the parasites of provocation, who exist only to feed from the profits of their own uncaring mind. And fall not victim to hatred-filled attempts, which may bring you undeserved messages from a realm beyond. Reach out only with compassion and curiosity, search for another's needs rather than your own, attempt to bear another's burden, and walk in their footsteps and then you will know and feel, only then will you have morally achieved. There is a moral or virtuous conduct that must prevail if we are to succeed in what we endeavor to achieve. I choose morality over provocation!

I Do!

WHY DO WE do what we do when we do? Why do we put in the long, arduous, and extreme hours of work trying to achieve our goals in the paranormal field? Why do we even attempt to make the effort? I would have to say we do it because it matters, because it is important! I always believe that we do these things because they really do matter and that all of us, in a combined effort, can make the difference in the paranormal community. Thus, avoiding falling prey to the heady nature of praise and the slippage between it and our success differentiates those of us who are truly doing this for the right reasons and continue to do so to this very day. Our exploration into the unknown can become overwhelming at times, yet we press forward. We can fall victim to mindless attacks from those who do not believe, yet we press forward. We are not characters in a story, and neither are those we search out, though they may have stories to share with us at times. It is up to us to distinguish between what truly is paranormal and that which is not, and as we do, we need to combine our efforts and gain some understanding of these occurrences. Do we yet truly understand these unknown and eerie images we encounter? Do we know why they dwell within the darkest crags and mysterious shadowlike worlds? Do we have what it takes to even begin to understand the complexity of what may be part of an unknown realm? Do we have the resolve to continue our journey to the very end? As for myself, I can answer this simply by saying, I do, I do, I do, and in conclusion, I must genuinely say, I do!

THE CLEANSING RITUAL!

MOST PARANORMAL GROUPS have bonded among one another within their own team dynamics and work well together. But it is a sad reality that some members of the team may have lost that fire and passion they possessed from the very start. Remember the excitement, the fire, and passion that each member had in the beginning? It was the bond that held everyone together and was shared by all. All too often, you will come across those who choose to join in whenever they feel it serves their purpose and not for the team. Some members will even use an investigation solely as a social gathering place, much like a neat little social club where they can do whatever they please, totally ignoring the real reason and vision set out in the beginning! Don't get me wrong; camaraderie is a good thing, but not when it begins to affect what we do and attempt to achieve in this field. My view here is this: when a team is formed and develops within itself toward a goal and contains the passion and fire to attain that goal, there is no stopping them. But when a select few opt to make it a social gathering place or, even worse, join in only when it suits them or involves a more popular location, it really pisses me off! Not only have they lost the true meaning of a purpose, but they have also now begun affecting others within the team. Of course, we don't become neglectful on purpose. Who wakes up and says, "Oh yeah, I guess today will be the day that I should drop my passion for the paranormal, now it's just for fun"? No, that doesn't happen. But what is very real is that some most often do get caught in what they consider a boring routine, and the passion slowly fades away. We all enjoy the camaraderie of like-minded people who share similar characteristics and interests. We understand that in every life situation, cliques form based on race, religion, economic class, and work. In every imaginable situation, likes and dislikes, alliances and exclusions form. But when it comes to the point of affecting other members of the team, we as leaders need to make the decision. It is time for a paranormal cleansing. Remove the negativity from the group and move on! Remember why we are all in this. Do it for the right reasons and do not let the drama from others affect the greater cause. Do not allow others within your team to confine you or others of the team to this negative place. What we attempt to achieve in this complex and multilayered field has no room for thrill seekers or social gatherings. Send them on their way along with their aloof mystique for social visits and find others who share the passion and vision for finding answers. If we are trying so hard to cope with this mess for our team's sake, then we are not supporting our members who are willing to continue on. Teamwork should be a positive experience, not fraught with tension and strategizing. So if you are experiencing this within your team dynamics, take out the bucket and soap. It's time for a cleansing!

WHEN SILENCE FALLS

WHEN SILENCE FALLS upon our waiting ears and the shadows begin to stir in the night, what risks do we as paranormal groups face? Risks will always be with us and are an integral part of what we do and what we are attempting to achieve in this field. Even the simplest form of investigative practices can open us up and leave us vulnerable to, well, let's just say, "something not so nice" from a place we still know very little about. What other factors are involved in our endeavors? Just how many risks do we actually take day to day as we seek out that which may be? It's a given that there will always be the risk of failing, the risk of not being able to help a client to fully understand what may be occurring in their home, or even the risk of physical injury due to our surroundings. But when we consider for a moment the risk of spiritual and emotional injuries that may befall us, risk management takes on a whole new meaning! No human can truly understand the complexity of this unknown realm, nor can we even fathom the possibilities of what may be lurking in the shadows when silence falls. We all have different views and beliefs on how to protect ourselves when we set out and endeavor contact from beyond, but how can we know it truly works? Diverse religious beliefs drive us to opt for many different forms of protection, but at the same time, there are those who may not base their decisions upon a religious belief at all and do just fine during their encounters in the night. So based solely on this information, do you think there is something within each of us, something of our own individual will, our very soul and spirit, or maybe even an inner strength, that protects us? It's a debate worth having, and each and every one of us will defend our own beliefs to the end. But in the end, it is our individual and personal beliefs that will determine how we choose to face that which lurks in the darkness, and none of us will be wrong in our choices. This is not an attempt for a baited religious debate by any means. My purpose here is to acknowledge the inner strength each and every one of us possesses, which I believe to be an invaluable weapon in our arsenal as we continue our journey when silence falls!

OF SPIRIT AND OF SOUL

A S I SEEK out those who may be, who is it from within that does watch me? From another realm, dark and cold, haunting and elusive, who is it that may dwell here in this place? Is it the spirit of one who passed long ago now draped by the shadows, concealed by night, and imprisoned by nightmares unimaginable? Or maybe a poor soul who has lost its way, left wandering, searching, and wanting for the touch of another for just any glimmer of light that can guide them to their final destination? Are there angels that walk among you and watch over you? Do they watch you from a place I cannot see, celestial in their being and divine in their purpose? Or is there a dark and malevolent presence lurking in the blackness, waiting for me as I walk on the very edge of some maddening and hidden abyss, lying in wait for no other reason but to pull me into a hell-like existence with it? This be my journey, this be my reason to venture onward and seek out, to embark on a voyage into an unknown place—a place riddled with secrets, a place laden with mystery and painted with wonders, as if a masterpiece of the mind. Within me resides a dream, there lives longing and hope, a hope to finally see and a hope to understand. Through my own aspirations and beliefs, through desire and faith, through my conviction and determination, I will trek forward. My passion will define me, my devotion will drive me, and my hunger and thirst for knowledge shall guide me. So with a pretentious yearning and unrelenting want, I shall continue to endeavor to succeed in my search. And if this unknown and mysterious realm is meant to remain unseen, then why has it not been cloaked from the eyes of all? This not being an essence of the truth, for the clues still remain and the messages seen, a path has been set. The question remaining within dimensions unknown and inhabited of spirit and soul. My quest will continue to journey's end. Of spirit and of soul? My answer is yes, for those within and for my own!

A PARANORMAL BEAUTY

T O SEE IT in one's own mind, to feel it in one's very soul, and to be drawn in by its true essence and beauty. There is an alluring and haunting call that resounds through the calm and peacefulness of night. There is an orchestrated artistry that reaches to embrace me. Shadows and sounds echo throughout as if to charm me and share its long-hidden and silent story. There is a certain elegance within this unknown realm, taunting and inviting me to become part of its very existence, part of its history. The enchanting still, obscured in blackness, touches your very soul. Blinded by the night, seeing only the haunted images within my mind, I notice the picturesque beauty and shared imagery as it appears resplendent and hypnotic. All obscured yet seen of the soul, all hidden yet felt of the spirit has become magnificent as it embraces the heart. Souls of the night, angels within a realm, dark spirits of malevolent intent now entice me and draw me in by their mystery and beauty. Perhaps it is a divine meaning transcended before me to understand? I may never know, but in dead silence, there can be heard the enchanting and harmonious melody as it moves through you, nostalgic and bewitching is its caressing breeze and gentle touch. There is a beauty in the night, a beauty that beckons, a hidden and mysterious beauty that is both alluring and haunting. Such is the temptress that dwells within, such is her paranormal beauty.

WRAPPED IN THEIR WINGS

ARE THERE REALLY angels that walk among us? In my heart I believe it to be true. The echoes can be heard as they resound a message of their presence. For those that miss loved ones who have long passed, for those that reach out to touch the hearts of others in need of care, for those who spread love and kindness and share the warmth of their own souls, therein lies your angel. Endless hurt yielded by an unrelenting world shall be vanquished; sorrowful tears that flow gently from loving eyes will be wiped away by the wings of your angel. A divine messenger and celestial being, so filled with the true spirit of light this very day, watches over you. Believe in the light of their heavenly halos, believe in the warmth and the tenderness of their loving wings, and believe in the harmonious song carried from their melodious harps and delivered directly to your very soul. You may feel lost in an uncaring and seemingly cruel world, you may be saddened by events in your life, or an overwhelming emptiness may have you in its grasp. Worry not, for if you believe that your angel is with you and sheds tears as you do, you will be lifted from the sadness and from your sorrow. You need not see their physical presence, for they are with you everlasting. There is an infinite love and never-ending compassion that surrounds your very spirit and resides within the soul. Let their glowing warmth and light embrace you. Share in the reverence you believe is offered and be nurtured by the thought of their very being. If you feel happiness from just the thought of an angel, if you are comforted in the belief of their existence, if the hurt in your life is lessened by the hope and wish of their very being, then I say to you, angels do walk among us! Keep believing and keep the hope alive as your guardian angel holds you warm. Just the belief alone will empower you as you remain wrapped in their wings.

PARANORMAL RECIPE FOR SUCCESS

WHATEVER OUR GOALS may be as paranormal investigators, there are some inner qualities and powers that are required for their achievement. Remember, our success is not only something that will be a spectacular event for us but will also set the pace for future researchers to learn from and to follow. When we examine our ambitions, our desires, and our goals in a very sincere way, we may discover that, to our amazement, we really can accomplish amazing things when we fully apply ourselves. With some people in our field, they become stagnant in their beliefs and research and just settle for what is. I believe this is because familiarity brings them a sense of comfort and security. With myself and a lot of others out there, we choose to step out of the comfort zone and apply ourselves completely as we continue our search for answers. Below, I have listed the ingredients we need to create this paranormal recipe for success.

1. The ability to decide exactly what you want to achieve
2. A strong desire and kind, feeling soul
3. Visualization of a goal
4. Willpower
5. Self-discipline
6. Persistence and care
7. Compassion and respect
8. Teamwork and unity
9. Drive and focus
10. A sincere passion and love for what you do!

Combine all the above ingredients together in one extra large heart, mind, and soul. Stir in a touch of diversity and a dash of willingness to stay the path. Give this mixture a heavy dusting of caring emotions and let stand for a lifetime, and you will see that you have created a culinary masterpiece and one very genuine and dedicated individual on their way to success.

PARANORMAL MIND-SET

I N THE FIELD of paranormal research, we use our five senses more than ever in our search for answers. However, these fundamental features are sometimes unable to assist us in making concrete decisions with regard to things that cannot be seen or explained by logical thinking and then present it as a proof. Approaching the paranormal from a research perspective is often difficult because of the lack of acceptable physical evidence we collect as determined by today's society. Most of today's society believes that the paranormal or spiritual world does not conform to conventional expectations of nature and what it has taught us. Thus, with that stubborn mind-set, people become overly skeptical and unwilling to accept the possibility of its existence and write off any findings as ever being legitimate. I mean, listen, we carry around this three-pound mass of material in our heads, which controls every single thing we will ever do for a reason. From enabling us to think, learn, create, and feel emotions, it controls every blink, each breath, and every heartbeat experienced during our lifetime. This wondrous control center is our brain. It is a structure so amazing and complex in itself, and we use only a fraction of its capabilities. The hidden potentials of our mind are more startling than the wonders of nature and the marvelous achievements of human talents and thought. I have myself developed what I like to call a paranormal mind-set, or an open-mindedness to all possibilities in this life and the hereafter. I believe a dark and mysterious realm exists or even another dimension where spirits may possibly wander. I am focused on finding answers to the "why" rather than "It does not exist, never has, never will" attitudes. As we experience and learn from our interactions with the paranormal, we begin to see and start to open and understand the possibilities that our mind has with enabling us to be better at what we do as researchers.

Our minds are strong and their potential endless. It is what determines the course of our individual lives; it is our deeply held beliefs, passions, values, fears, hopes, worries, attitudes, and desires. I have a paranormal mind-set, and I will continue to develop it and learn from it. The key to understanding the phenomena we experience in relation to paranormal events is the mind. Don't have a closed one, open up a little, and begin to see things in a different light!

ODE TO THE PARANORMAL INVESTIGATOR

FOR THE CONSTANT sacrifices each of you make from day to day. For your determination and stick-to-it attitudes. For your willingness to enter a dark and confusing world in search of answers. For the hours and days you dedicate to trying to understand a realm filled with mystery and hidden secrets. For dealing with the adversity and skepticism that face you like a tormenting and unrelenting storm, yet you remain a force to be reckoned with. For showing compassion toward a soul lost and searching for light. For building that bridge over the vast and bottomless abyss of doubt. For embracing your teams and the diversity each of them possesses. For taking that first step and then continuing your journey to discovery no matter the obstacles laid out before you. For pursuing your dream and staying on the path. For your thirst for knowledge and reason. For acknowledging that you do possess untapped abilities deep within you that will help you strive toward that one common goal. For not settling for the past but learning from it instead. For building that road for others to travel on in the future. For trusting in your heart to guide you and to show you the way. For being yourself in a world that changes and where newer understandings have become a thing of the past. For remaining enthusiastic in your beliefs and realizing the true magic it can bring to you. I thank all of you, from the bottom of my heart, who continue the search for answers others fear. For all that you do, for all that you dream, for all that you encounter along the way, you can take pride in what you have set out to accomplish. I will stand at your side the entire trek, and I am proud to be a part of this paranormal investigators family! What a wondrous journey we face together, what a wondrous thing!

I WAIT

THEIR PICTURES STILL remain upon these cobweb-covered walls and are strewn across these dusty and year-worn floors. A child's torn and tattered shoe lies on its side, as if it had just been kicked off a tiny little foot. Their physical existence was snuffed away like the wick of a smoldering candle, no longer to fill these rooms with laughter or with tears. Somewhere hidden within these walls, within these floors and rooms, a child's first steps were taken, a love was shared, a sorrow was felt, and lives were shared and celebrated. There were times she cried at night and begged the whispering darkness to tell her why. There were times when he cried tears of joy and happiness as he held his family deep within his heart and soul. Now that they have passed, is their story held within these walls, yearning to find a kind soul to share it with? I reach out to touch these walls and pull back from the coldness and hardness of a soulless stone. I wonder about and feel for those that created the light and warmth that once were a living presence in this home. For when love in this physical world dies, it is not in a moment of angry battle, nor is it when fiery bodies lose their heat of passion for life. It is when a family loved, a family shared, and a life filled these now-empty passages. The love remains; it lies in wait, waiting for someone to be audience to its performance in the night. So patiently, compassionately, and respectfully, I wait!

PARA-UNITY:
THE REALIZATION

PARANORMAL UNITY! SOUNDS great, doesn't it! Why is it then that recently we are just starting the push for it? It has always been my belief that as paranormal groups, we have shared and practiced unity since day one. So why now is it so important to embrace it by joining a group specifically named for unity? I think not; unity has always existed between our groups, and those that choose to embrace it and learn from it will reap in its benefits. The past year could be read as one in which the realization between paranormal groups was to focus on unity and diversity. Yet there are so many groups out there who stand against the unity that could be shared between them and others within their region or even globally. I still believe to this very day that these groups have placed themselves upon a pedestal and consider themselves holier-than-thou. In past attempts to bring our cooperative efforts together and focus on achieving goals, it fell upon deaf ears as the arrogance of these groups led them to believe they were better than the rest. The deadly dilemma of our day is that the assertion of one's own distinctiveness seems too easily to imply attacking others' beliefs simply because they differ, ignoring and destroying all bonds of unity, thereby destroying the very roots of their sense of unity with others. So I think to myself often, must the coming year be a replay of the last or, worse still, be marked by the collapse of mutual respect, the destruction of others' values, virtues, and beliefs? I wholeheartedly choose to use diversity as a strength and empower the unity that has always been shared between us. There is no specific need to prequalify for some page or group claiming unity that will decide whether or not you are worthy of their time and are selected to join only because you meet their specifications. Focus on the things we have already accomplished and are striving for each and every day. We have always worked in unity; there are just those who choose not to. New horizons are in our futures, and they are bright. Be inspired and reach out with respect to others who want to share the knowledge and are ready to make the difference. Continually strive to develop trust, cooperation, and the mutual respect with and for your colleagues. Listen, it's not a secret society, it's not an elite group, and it most definitely is not a status symbol or popularity contest. Paranormal unity is something we have shared in for years, and those of us who do it the right way and for the right reasons are the ones that will make the difference!

FAILURE IS AN OPTION!

I F YOU WERE to put me on the spot and ask me, "What one thing do you find the hardest to deal with as a paranormal investigator?" my answer, without hesitation, would be "failure." This is more than likely the reason most will not even attempt to try different things in the field of research or even to start their very own investigative team; they are just too afraid of failing. I mean, just the fact that you believe you will fail even before you have tried will not get you anywhere in life. There are those out there who from time to time will come up with totally brilliant ideas but worry about failing before they even get off the ground. They tend to worry about what others may think or how it may look in the end if they fail at what they attempt to achieve. I know that this shouldn't play any role in whatever I do as an investigator basically because the only person that it matters to is me. But boy, do I get this overwhelming feeling of embarrassment and failure when something goes belly up. Most will even toss in the towel as soon as things become difficult or they come face-to-face with certain obstacles and adversity. This clouds their minds with negativity, and even the simplest solution will remain hidden from them for that fact alone. You hear it all the time: "Failure is not an option!" I call bullshit on that one as I believe that our failures make us stronger as we learn from them. Attempting to be a perfectionist is a valiant thing but generally implausible in this field because there are so many unknowns. When you actually think about it, nothing in life is a definite, and we will always face hardships along the way. Just prepare yourself to deal with the negativity you may face along the way. After all, is it not better to have started and failed at something than not try at all? Our failing is a learning process. Do not let anyone tell you different because I say, failure is an option!

DO YOU HAVE CHANGE FOR A DREAM?

YOU KNOW AS well as I do that each and every one of us experiences change in our lives, especially in what we attempt to achieve in the paranormal field. Change is the one constant in our lives that we can count on, and that's how it will always be. Some changes we look forward to, and others we fear. When we come face-to-face with change, we have but two choices that we can make. We can sit in despair of change, or we can choose to deal with it and learn and grow from it. Change is unavoidable in this field; we must always face change, but at the same time, we must continue our dreams and our passions to find some sort of explanation and proof of paranormal existence. Though you may think your dream is far-reaching in this field, it is still your dream! With constant change, your dream of finding these answers will begin to eventually manifest before your very eyes. The dreams we have as individuals give our lives meaning and inspire us to continue no matter what obstacles may come. We all dream to some extent about the change we strive for in the paranormal community. We dream about change and improvement as we set goals—seemingly impossible goals. Goals will challenge us now and in the future, but it is the dream that will drive us forward. I like to think that we are all intelligent beings; therefore we know within us that something is out there that does defy logic and possesses a deeper meaning to our existence in this realm and that of another after we reach our final sleep. Humanity lives on dreams; it yearns for inspiration! So if you come to that door and it has been shut before you by the ridicule and doubt of others, if the curse of mankind in today's society has released attacks of arrogance and self-proclaimed superior egos, I have but one thing to say to you. Reach out and turn the knob. If it still doesn't open, kick it the—down and continue your journey forward. Your dream is there for you to follow. Do not let others be the means of its destruction. If you need to create your own change, make it follow your dream!

PERCEPTIONS OF INTERPRETATION

T HOUGH WE ALL perceive and interpret things in diverse and different ways, would you not agree that it somehow leads us in the same direction as we all attempt to make sense of things that occur in the paranormal realm? When we look at the human soul, for instance, we know that it is part of the physical shell we now inhabit, but once our physical vessel has taken that final breath and the soul is believed to move on into another realm, how do we perceive it then? As we gather evidence in an attempt to prove a paranormal existence, we will all perceive and interpret it in many different ways based on our own beliefs and values. Just one example I would like to throw out there would be the Bible. This is in no manner or form said to create a religious debate but only a statement to validate a point. When you consider that the Bible consists of numerous and wondrous events, it has been rewritten throughout history by many different people, in many different languages, throughout various continents over approximately 1,600 years. Now here is my point: interpretations and perceptions of the written word had to have been affected by personal beliefs and values somewhere down the line, creating our own diverse beliefs in today's society, even though the same message is there. Now back to the task. A lost soul in the afterlife seen at times in human form and donned in clothing of an era once lived. Why? Bodily features recognized that also resemble the state it occupied in the physical realm. The ability to speak, to see, to respond at times intelligently to our very queries. The physical body, now laid to rest, was the host to eyes, ears, heart, brain, and many other physical aspects. So the question remains: when we see something from another realm, why does it still reveal itself in such a way, possessing the abilities of sight, thought, and physical interaction? We believe there is an energy in which soul and spirit may utilize to move and/or materialize, but the physical attributes of any apparition we may capture, there is our quandary. Interpretation and perception in an ever-changing world causes us to see things in different ways, and as we attempt to understand them, a belief is created. So when we encounter something within the shadows, are we seeing it from our own perception and interpretation, or is it an actuality of what the anomaly possesses within an afterlife? The natural existence of the body versus the supernatural existence of the visual presence of such, which may remain in an afterlife—it's mind-boggling! Is our mind then controlled in some way, used as a canvas for something supernatural to paint the images that we see? This will always cause me to wonder as I remain perplexed and fascinated by it. This is why I continue my search and will always allow my perceptions and interpretations to remain flexible and ever changing. Will you?

At The Crossroads

J UST HOW MANY lost souls wander through a vast, empty, and
cold darkness? We will never know for sure how and why this
event may occur. During our experiences as investigators, we trek
through rooms and passages devastated by time and aged by years long
past. We witness hints and shreds of moonlight as it creeps through
tattered and worn windows yet never fully reaches the blackness within.
It is still and silent, and the air seems to have suffered a death in itself.
There are no more whispers, no more laughter, only an eerie silence
that embraces our very being. Yet at times, souls linger, which may
experience sadness, sorrow, and heartbreak and may convey their
despair to those willing to listen. Wandering in the shadows and in
search of any light, could there possibly be good and kind souls that
have become trapped by something dark and malevolent, blocking any
hope of moving on? And if this be the case, could there be a place
where enlightenment and darkness intertwine on the journey hereafter,
a crossroad, if you will? Imagine good and evil in an afterlife with
two distinct paths, but the battle that rages between these two forces
has allowed the evil side to manipulate the journey of the good. In
every nook and cranny of our earthly existence, the battle is waged
between good and evil, and once we pass, I believe it to continue on.
At this so-called crossroad, something with malicious intent looks for a
weakness and awaits to exploit and feed from it. If such an entity really
exists, it really doesn't matter at all whether we think it's harmful to
conceive of evil in this way, or if we think we would be more at peace
with ourselves if we just ignore the idea of an entity behind the evil,
or if we think that humankind should just grow out of it. What does
matter is the possibility that it does exist, and in our everyday life or in

an afterlife, the time will come when we come to that crossroad where good and evil will cross paths. Use compassion when you attempt to communicate to these wandering souls, for in their realm, the light of day has been removed and their path has been blocked. So look both ways when you come to your crossroad!

ORBALICIOUS?

A FTER VIEWING SOME recent programs related to the paranormal, I have seen numerous accounts of people claiming "spirit orbs" in their photographs. It seems like every one of them claim this to be an actual manifestation of an entity from another realm, and no other explanation is given during the show as to other possibilities. Though some orbs out there may be unexplainable and the possibility of something paranormal in nature could be a factor, we have to realize that a majority of what we see are of natural causes. I have had numerous photos sent to me personally from individuals interested in the paranormal and have seen these shows. I have responded to most with logical explanations for their pictures. It is when the digital camera first became popular that this phenomenon began to emerge. It is the nature of these cameras to reveal many objects in the form of what some believe to be ghostly transparent orbs. Most believe that since they were not able to see the anomaly with the naked eye yet they mysteriously appear on the photo, the conclusion is drawn that it must be paranormal. Now don't get me wrong; I do believe that there are instances in which we may capture something paranormal in nature, but these events are few and far between. One of my beliefs is that a true spirit orb should generate its own light source or energy field, thus being visible to the naked eye and even leaving its own trails as it moves about. The most common explanation for this phenomenon is basic and simple, and I only state this for those out there who may not know as of yet—they are merely a matter of dust, moisture, insects, or other foreign material that becomes visible after reflecting the flash or other light source within the area. In an article published by the Association for the Scientific Study of Anomalous Phenomena, these orbs that appear on photographs are actually "circles of confusion" no matter what shape they may take. The cause, most likely, would refer back to the object being out of focus or a blurry highlight due to its proximity to the camera lens and flash. These vital and most important facts are always left out of the equation when orchestrated for a television series, and I just wanted those who may be a novice or just starting out to know what you may face down the line. I myself believe that ghostly spirit orbs do exist, but with so many out there that post it as definite proof, it has become taboo for investigative groups to post for the sole reason of instant nonbelief. I still wait for the day that an orb will stop directly in front of my face and say, "Hey, Gary, I am a spirit orb. Nice to meet you!" Until then, I can only hope to find concrete proof of their existence. However, I will still post these anomalies for your review and your opinions. Thanks!

THE PARANORMAL DIFFERENCE!

W HILE PURSUING OUR goal as paranormal investigators, we must continue to do so with certain and sustaining determination. This tool alone can repel discouragement and doubt with ease. Sometimes we find ourselves distracted from our central goal by other desires. We get overwhelmed by obstacles, ridicule, isolation, fatigue, and even failure. At these times, determination can push us onward and give us the energy to overcome. By keeping us on a path, determination helps us to turn our visions into realities and to live by our own values. In order to empower our drive and determination, we must also possess a willpower like no other. Is the method that today's society views the present state of the universe and the possibility of another realm within it the way we should all view it? I say no most defiantly! I possess a willpower and the determination to think out of the box and will hold this true until my dying day. There is no such creature as he who is all-knowing in the paranormal community, no matter what you may hear. It is an ongoing learning process shared by many and will continue to the end of time. We are here now, and we can make the difference now as we come together and gather the knowledge among us. Our basic thought processes and beliefs in our research are not set in stone but are more apt to change as we learn more about why things occur within a realm we do not fully understand. Yet there will always exist uncertainty; there will always exist ridicule and doubt. We will always deal with the arrogance of others who claim to know it all, but through our determination and willpower, we will overcome those obstacles and be better off for it. Do not, for one minute, believe that your destiny is predetermined by a stagnant society, nor has it been set by heredity or your environment! It is you that can change how this unknown realm is viewed, and it is you that can make the difference. If we accept the argument and assume human behavior as a consequence of external factors rather than of free will and choice, then we must realize that our explanation of human behavior leaves no room for our own morality. Embrace your determination. Sustain the willpower that is part of your very spirit, your very soul. Through this, your vision will become clearer, your passion will radiate like no other, and you will continue your journey with a much clearer view of the path ahead. Myself? I'm moving forward and hope to bump into you along the way!

WITH RESOUNDING RESILIENCE

WITHOUT FAIL, DAY in and day out, I hear it: "Give it up. You'll never find the answers you're looking for and will fail in proving paranormal existence." It really makes you wonder sometimes. What is it that each of us possesses that keeps us going in this field of research? I for one can truly state that it is our resilience. In our field of study, it takes a lot for us to adapt to our misfortunes and setbacks. When we are resilient in our purpose, we harness that inner strength that eventually helps us to overcome these overwhelming challenges. I use it to free myself from dwelling on the problems I face in a society that is prone to settle for the norm as they deem it. I choose not to fall victim to a so-called social vulnerability. Don't get me wrong; resilience will not make the problems magically fade away. But it does give us the ability to see past them and strive to achieve something much bigger. Adversity is a major foe in our dealings among the paranormal community and those that choose not to believe altogether. Face it and stand resilient at all times, for it is adversity that will strengthen you. Let adversity become your stepping stone and not an obstacle during your journey for truth! It just seems easier sometimes to assimilate to popular beliefs, if only to avoid confrontation and ridicule. I have opted to not fall into this category and feel sorry for those that have. Our world is comprised of many different people diverse in their ways and in their beliefs. And what is successful for one group may not work for another. If everyone lived and believed in the same way, we would be mindless identical drones with no real purpose. Do not be swayed by the critical opinions of others who will attempt to bring you down to their level. Remain resilient in the face of adversity and doubt; it's what will sustain you as you venture forward in your research. Remain unique, remain resilient in your endeavors, and in doing so, you will all benefit from it in the end. If there is one thing that can eventually unite us in the paranormal field, it is that we are all different. And it's that difference and our resilience that will allow us to grow and learn not only about ourselves but about the answers we so desperately seek. So with resounding resilience, I will always remain determined and focused!

REALM OF CURIOSITY

THEY SAY THAT curiosity killed the cat, but last time I checked, we are human, and thus, the statement does not apply. As paranormal investigators, curiosity is an essential quality that we possess and that drives us socially, morally, and even intellectually. Throughout history, it is our curious nature that has led us to a higher purpose and to apply deeper meaning of things that occur in the paranormal realm. In simpler terms, it is what makes us move beyond that which seems apparent or what society deems the norm. Our curiosity compels each and every one of us to find reason and meaning to what may exist in an afterlife. While we trek forward on our path of instinctive curiosity, we find a void where questions about the events that take place either in our physical world or the unknown world that may exist yet remains hidden. Nevertheless, we remain focused and determined, for it is our curiosity and our commitment to it that will eventually lead us to answers in a realm we do not yet fully understand. It is this very element that will sustain our passion, our enthusiasm, and our determination to continue forward and find answers, the answers others may fear. Our curiosity then becomes our hunger and our need to explore this other side, this unknown realm, this place seemingly concealed by shadows. I have an overpowering curiosity and consider it healthy because it causes me to listen to others along the way. Every morsel of information and knowledge that I can acquire from anybody can only add to my ever-growing learning process. All of us that share in the passion of the paranormal have a wide and diverse range of characteristics and attributes. Some are innate, some are formed through our experiences, and others are developed through wisdom and deep insight. But the most important driving factor that I would have to say is our curiosity. It leads us to wonder, and when we wonder, we begin to ponder the possibilities that eventually help us to learn. Will we ever fully understand the events we deal with that seem to emit from another dark and unknown realm? In this physical world, I think not. But let your curiosity be your guide. Let it lead you to attain your desires and goals. Use it to create your visions and your dreams. As we embrace our individual curiosity, we gain insights to things hidden, and the learning process continues. So it is through this that our shared knowledge and experiences can make a difference in our studies. Wouldn't you say? Just curious!

FOCUS, PEOPLE!

O UR MIND IS a powerful and constant magnet, subconsciously picking up everything around it and processing it to the point where we can use it now or store the information for future interactions. It is important—no, it is vital—that we do not let negativity in our current lives or the past define our future. When others have said or done something that upsets you, accept the fact that you cannot change it, nor can you change them, and just move on. Reliving what happened yesterday only robs you of enjoying today and clouds your sight and focus on shaping what you can achieve tomorrow! Discipline your mind; use it to strengthen your commitment and your vision. Create your own destiny and do not let others block or lead you astray from your path. Focus on what you are striving to achieve and never neglect it for even a moment. Focus on your dreams and the journey that will eventually lead you to accomplishing them. Focus on the thought that it is you and only you that can make the choice to get up each day and face yourself and what lies before you with a positive attitude. So make the difference and focus, people!

SO WHAT!

A S WE ENDEAVOR to make headway in our paranormal research, we can be sure of one thing. Discouragement is always just around the corner and remains a constant we must deal with day to day. But it only takes a few words of inspiration to change our discouragement into revitalized hope. Progress just seems to become more difficult to achieve, and at times we are close to giving up on any idea or lose hope. Most of the time, we are tempted to take the path of least resistance, which just seems to make things easier, but what is the sense in that? Never settle for the norm! Think out of the box and remain resilient and determined in your efforts. One of the key problems with having so many issues to deal with and many opportunities for things to go wrong in the paranormal field is that we lose our sense of dedication, and thus, our hope and passion begin to fade. Today's society is reluctant to accept much of what we present as clues or proof of paranormal events as being valid for the sole reason that they are not ready for and generally fear change or knowledge of its existence. This should never deter you from your passion or cause you to lose focus! At times, it seems quite overwhelming and your goals nonobtainable. So what! We all need words of encouragement now and then, some inspiring thoughts to pick us up again! Be the one who makes the difference. Have the confidence to stand alone if necessary. Have the courage to make the tough decisions and the willingness to let those around you help. It takes courage and strength to continue your journey. Through the quality of your actions and the integrity of your intent, you will make the difference! It may be soon, it may come farther down the line, but one thing is certain: we will achieve that which we have set out to accomplish!

Paranormal Teamwork and Leadership

OKAY, WE ALREADY know about the challenges we face each and every day of our lives within the paranormal field. What is it exactly that distinguishes us as good leaders within our individual teams? We develop our teams for their ability to work together toward a common vision and goal. It is not a one-person show, and teamwork is crucial in what we endeavor to achieve. It means doing everything we physically and mentally can to accomplish anything! It is vital that our team members have a sense of belonging, if you will, a sort of joint action and cooperation in which each member sees the others as part of the attainment of goals. To put it in simpler terms, let's build a fire. We as leaders are the first log into the pit, and we ignite the spark of vision. Now as we fuel that flame with our team who are now invested in the same vision, the fire soon rages, and your initial spark has become a burning light like no other. Individuality does count, but it is the teamwork that will bring it all together. Have the mind-set that none of us are ever as good as all of us when we stand together. As I have stated numerous times in the past, it is vital that we embrace the diversities possessed by our team members. Respect their ideas, religious beliefs, views, and inputs no matter what. By doing this, they will understand and believe that thinking, planning, decisions and actions are better when done cooperatively. It will drive your team and enable them to contribute and accomplish more than you ever thought possible. We as leaders must always think in a team mind-set and stand by our team members 100 percent, no matter the circumstances. That is our responsibility as leaders, and I accept it in its entirety! First off, I disagree that great leaders are born and not made. I have been taught by my own team how to be an effective leader, and I thank them for that. Secondly, leadership is not about being liked; more importantly, it's about having a vision, a passion, and a determination to create the best and most effective environment for your team members, your peers, and for your clients, who become a vital part of your final product. Being an accomplished and true leader comes through creating a high-performance, high-value culture where your team is respected as individuals, challenged always, stretched beyond what seems unobtainable, and last but not least, recognized for their efforts. Listen to your team members, learn from them, respect them at all times, and never belittle them for it is them that make us. And it is them that can break us! A good leader creates a vision, a picture of what can be. A great leader can inspire every team member to work as one toward that common goal and do it proudly. With the proper leadership, adversity can become a motivation and driving force that will eventually highlight the true strengths and skills of your team. Be the leader they want and the leader that all your team members deserve to have!

SILENT ECHO OF WHISPERS

DO YOU EVER get to a point during an investigation that you stop and think, "This is just too damned quiet, nothing's happening, and I'm moving on"? I think we have all experienced this somewhere down the line. We become more focused on wanting to hear that audible response and become frustrated when all we have is the silence. It is the silence that you really need to embrace because within it, there is an inner peace and certain emptiness that echoes its mysterious whispers throughout. When you open your mind to the very essence of silence, you create a haunting and mystical union with self and the message it may have to share with you. You will find, at times, that a gentle inner peace and silence exists at that very moment, and it has always been there, waiting. And through it, stories can be heard. It really depends on you taking the time and making that extra effort to stop and listen to what silence has to say. As you allow it to surround you a serene stillness, an apparent void and seeming nothingness will begin to envelop you. Through this very silence, hidden whispers and echoes of audible essence can be heard as stories and haunting clues return to fall upon ears willing to listen. So at times, all that you seek and all that you hope for are merely contained within the silence. When the time is right and that which is veiled within the shadows seeks to communicate with anyone willing to listen, you will find that this mystical silence possesses more eloquence than speech itself. Souls lost and wandering, spirits seeking what they once held dear, entities lurking behind a curtain of darkness, angelic messages reaching out to us. No matter the case, never give up on the silence. Within it, you may find a harmonious and melodic message orchestrated just for you. Seek out not just the haunting sounds of the night. Embrace the silence, for within it awaits the echoes of whispers searching for a patient and willing ear!

LIFE'S HOPE

AHHHH, THE EXPERIENCES we encounter on a day-to-day basis during our lifetime! We have our struggles, we revel in our triumphs, and we look to one another for help and support along the lines. As human beings, when we encounter a challenge, we have the freedom to choose how we will react to it. Every decision that we make leads us down a different road, an unknown path, if you will. Though many of us will not arrive at exactly the same crossroads, one thing is for certain: the hope remains! The choices we make here in the paranormal field are a constant, reverberating echo of change. A change that we all strive for in the ways we share our knowledge and how we can all begin to learn from one another. None of us are ready to settle for the norm or what society views as the ordinary. We have a hope that we can find answers within the paranormal realm, and we allow this hope to drive and to sustain us throughout our life whatever our endeavors may be. We do not stand to the side and wait for the change to miraculously appear. We become the change. We become the hope! Hence, hope ignites a fire and strength within our very souls that bond us as one. There are those that give up along the way for the sole reason of frustration in not finding the answers. The search has been ongoing for millennia with little progress along the way, but just the word "progress" gives us the hope to continue. I look beyond the ridicule. I learn from the doubts of others. I turn my eyes toward the sky and continue my path. The answers are out there; they always have been, and they always will be. And when the shadows of our physical presence have vanished from this physical realm, guess what. We will have left our footprints for others that share the hope to continue following. Though tedious at times and overwhelming at others, our research is vital. So whether it's everyday life or what we strive to achieve as paranormal investigators, embrace the hope and empower your soul!

THEIR PLAYGROUND?

OST OF US believe that good souls and spirits may be lost
and possibly roam in a realm that, as of yet, we do not fully
understand. With that same belief, we know that something
dark and evil, which can enter and depart our realm whenever it desires,
also exists within this mysterious place. Is our physical world merely
a playground for these malicious beings? Are we considered their
"playthings" or subjects in a maniacal game of conquer the soul? I
believe that demons do walk among us daily and want nothing more
than to draw us into the darkness and suffering they have been sentenced
to decay in for eternity. So when we conduct our research into the
paranormal, we must remain vigil and take precautions at all times. For
us, it truly is not a game, but for these dark and malevolent creatures, we
are a prize as they desire nothing more than to devour our very souls and
hurt those we are close to. Anything demonic in nature can take on any
form and emit emotions that can fool us, drawing us even closer to the
edge of their world where suffering and torment rule. It is so difficult for
us to determine whether or not any evidence we capture is from a good
or evil entity, for the evil that lies in wait can mimic all that we believe
to be good. Be cautious because all luminous encounters in the night
are not always with good intention. Take the necessary precautions each
and every time you dare to step into the unknown. Do not be fooled by
the mimic, who will attempt to lead you to a dark side from where there
may be no return. They lie in wait, they play the game, and they plot
and scheme for an opening just for that one chance to pull you in and
devour your soul or to hurt those near to you. It's not a thrill ride, and it's
not a game; this is their playground, and we are their objects of desire.
Remain vigil at all times!

EMPTY WORDS, LET THEM BE

IN DAYS LONG past and times long forgotten, there existed a people who lived in a place that saw not the light of day. No one believed that the day would come that they would ever leave from out of this darkness and were thus destined to dwell within it for an eternity. One man who stood up among these people rose and stated thusly, "As you have borne yourselves, as is seemly, and not haughtily wanted for the hope of light, I will give you a glimmer so that ye may seeketh a path therein to." This being said, these poor souls accepted the man's words as a truth and rode on together to seek that of which he spoke. In this dark realm, they chanced upon a land where wars of words raged; a famine laden with doubt was left unfed, and a thirst for knowledge was forbidden to be sated. In this land, there reigned an evil and dark force whence had risen from the egos of self-rule! The weary travelers thought unto themselves, "Will this be the place we shall perish, for the scarcity is so great and the creature lurks to feed from our hopes?" The one who led the people shouted out with a melancholy cry, "Worry not, my friends, and deafen thy ears to the empty words spoken from ignorance and arrogance. Blind thy eyes so ye may not see the chaos they attempt to release. And now follow the light which layeth directly before you, seen now within their grasp, as these obstacles are ignored." So they went hither and began to realize that a resilient brightness was to befall them, and the winds of knowledge fell upon their faces. The shroud of darkness now behind them, they continued their journey for answers. These curious people of times past ventured forth where no man had laid steps before them. They ran toward their fate with open arms and minds, never to be hindered by those who doubted them. From this day on, they knew within them that whatever is of value and virtue has to be from the heart, and those who would choose to stand against them would fall. They are only words, guys. Empty words from empty and arrogant minds. Don't give them a second thought or let them deter you in any way. We still do and always will have the support of one another!

Thus, With Malicious Intent, The Bait Is Set

THERE ARE THOSE of us who stand on the positive side of paranormal research. We seek only to find proof and reason for the existence of another realm where spirit and soul may dwell. On that same note, there are those out there who seek only to ridicule and cast doubt upon all that we do, and they proceed to do so in an extremist sort of way. Here is where your defenses come into play. I do agree that a certain amount of skepticism is healthy and at times helps us to gain a better knowledge in what we do. But there are people that have nothing better to do than create havoc and chaos within the paranormal field for the sole reason of their own self-satisfaction. Do not fall prey to their baited words! We have to realize that there are people who are intolerant of those that differ from them and will always try to bring you down to their level. I guess it gives them a sense of belonging and power as they have lackeys climb on the wagon with them. This arrogance is often a reflection of limited life experiences and knowing that there are those of us who strive to gain a greater life experience, instilling in them the thought that we may have something over them. Thus, the only conclusion is to bait us with words of ridicule, which, when used just right, will pull us down to their level of ignorance and cause unrest within our sect. There are no words we can use to cause them to see it through our eyes because this alone would show vulnerability that they would rather remain hidden. I have seen some over-the-top pages out there where ignorance runs rampant and individuals gather for the sole reason of ridicule and argument. Do not be drawn in by their words as they bait you and sit in wait to feed from you. Ignore their words and continue your path; this is the one way that you will get to them, and it really eats at them. Do not, and I emphasize, do not give them the satisfaction of knowing that they have gotten to you. This personality type is basically frightened by ambiguity or, in simpler terms, something not cut-and-dried; thus, it becomes an imperfection and a lack of certainty for them, and they lose control. Let them revel in themselves and feed from one another as they compliment one another with undue credit. These individuals are not worth one second of our time or effort; do not become a victim of their empty circumstance and words of ridicule. They will look at your passion and willingness to defend your beliefs, and they will bait you for their own amusement as they entrap you in their war of empty words. Some lie in wait for you to come along; some are actually on the hunt and will come to you. Do not waste your time or energy because it will only feed their enormous and ignorant egos. We are here for a reason—to find answers! Shake off the leeches and continue your journey!

COMING SOON

THEY WERE A ragtag team of misfits brought together and united for one purpose: to find the answers others feared! Devastating at times, sad and challenging at others, and even hilarious are their adventures as they endeavor a journey—a journey into the unknown! The future will test the limits of their resilience. Mysterious and moving, almost spiritual in its strangeness, this saga will bring this diverse group of paranormal researchers closer than ever imagined as they embrace a passion and vision as one. They will share their eerie, touching, and universal story of walking with the shadows and their haunting attempt at communication with souls lost within another realm! They are forced to make choices that will change their lives forever. As they give their all in their research, an intricate web is woven, which seems at times to entangle them. Knowing they stand as one, they realize they can accomplish unexpected things, wondrous and amazing things. With focus and determination, with serious reflection on issues beyond the superficial limits of conflict, this small and dedicated group of people joins together and journey into darkness to find that which is hidden within. Join them on their journey as they walk with the shadows! Coming to an investigation site near you!

EVERYBODY HAS ONE!

WHETHER IT IS based on your personal beliefs, values, background, or even experiences, we all have our own opinions about things we deal with on a daily basis. To break it down quite simply, an opinion is a subjective belief and usually the result of emotion or interpretation of facts. And let me be the first to say here that opinions are never right or wrong but merely figments of what each of us may believe to be true in one way or another. In today's society, we all express our own opinions in the many dealings we have in our personal interactions with others. I will notice that on occasion, an individual's opinion falls victim to violent attack, solely on the basis that someone else's opinion differs from theirs. There is really no justification for this and absolutely no basis for it. I respect others' opinions whether they match mine or are totally opposite from them. I learn from others in this respect and try to understand how they come to the conclusions that they do. And though, at times, I may sharply disagree with some, I take the extra step to try and learn exactly what it is I am disagreeing with in the first place. Beneficial indeed as I have actually changed my own opinion in regard to this process! We will deal with arrogant fools and downright fanatics constantly in life that are just so set in their ways that change is not an option. In my opinion, that makes us the wiser of the group for respecting, learning, and trying to understand the opinions of others. I am grateful for opinions shared here, though some may be more superficial than others. I am benefited by the thought processes that eventually are born from them. To attack or attempt to silence the opinion of others is just another example of ignorance we deal with daily. Do not, by any means, let the ignorance of others deter you from expressing your opinion! If you do, it will only deprive you and others from an opportunity to learn more or gain additional information and knowledge in our trek forward as we continue our journey to find answers. And that, my friend, is just my opinion!

NOW, IT'S PERSONAL

NO, EVERYONE, I'M not talking about some blatant personal attack, nor am I referring to my own deep-rooted, deep-seated, and esoteric beliefs. The point I am trying to make here involves the things that we attempt to present as far as evidence is concerned. Whether you choose to post EVPs, pictures, videos, or, God forbid, the ever-so-controversial orb, you fall victim to an onslaught of negativity from those who choose not to believe. The "personal" that I am talking about is our personal experiences during an investigation that completes the story to all other evidence we may have captured. When someone does not add this factor into the formula, they are only donning their own personal blinders. I don't know why there are those out there who just choose this forum as a place to come and ridicule others in their efforts. With some, I know for a fact it is just ignorance and a game. For others, it's arrogance and conceit with that extra dose of contempt and pomposity! Then there are those who really do consider themselves all-knowing and experts in the paranormal. As I have always stated in the past, none of us are really experts, and we all have much to learn in this field. We should take the opportunity and learn from one another. When I see someone else's posts as evidence and they ask for opinions, I will give an honest opinion that is measured and determined only from my experiences. We cannot truly tell them it is real or not due to the fact that we were not there with them, and we did not have the personal experiences that they alone witnessed, which adds validity to their claims. Our personal experiences during any investigation drives us to the conclusions that we each consider something valid. Others cannot see this and thusly cannot make any logical call, in my opinion. Remain resilient in your efforts and always consider this when you are faced with the negativity of others. Always know that there are those of us out there that do this for the right reasons and will always emote a well-deserved respect. As for the others, pity them as they will be stuck in a place they are happy to grow stagnant in. This is not, in any way, meant for the skeptics out there. I do learn from them as they at least factor in reasoning and science to come to their conclusions. This is meant for the "pot-stirrers," who have no other reason but to feed their own egos. Respect for our colleagues and knowing the importance of one's dignity is truly the mark of a great human being. I remember reading this a long time ago and still believe it to be true today: "To be one, to be united is a great thing. But to respect the right to be different is maybe even greater." Always consider the personal experiences that may have been involved when you look at something next time.

ONE FOUNDER'S BELIEF

BEING THE FOUNDER of a paranormal group and hopefully a good leader for my team, I have many thoughts and experiences that have helped develop my beliefs. I have come to the conclusion that as most people's experiences are subjective, you will find many stories and not a lot of what today's society would consider proof as far as captured evidence of paranormal existence. I find there to be three discernable levels of belief: those who believe and have themselves experienced the paranormal, those who have not had any type of ghostly encounters but still believe their existence to be true, and those who choose not to believe regardless of what they may have experienced. I myself would definitely fall into the first category. Proof to others, though nice, really does not affect me in any way. I have experienced the proof firsthand and want to learn more about these poor souls that exist in the shadows and are concealed in darkness. Are there those of us, who, just by our beliefs, have been drawn into this field by some mysterious force, or do our personal beliefs draw us to it? Change is occurring each and every day in what we do. Sure, a lot of "orb" footage is dust or other anomalies, but do not let that deter you from posting and asking the opinions of others. Those of us that do believe will look with an open mind. And by no means should you discard these as the possibility of them being more than just that of natural causes still exists. Who knows, this may have been a method used to disguise themselves in the spiritual realm because they know that's how we will interpret it! I know for a fact that I do not have all the answers and maybe never will, but I do believe we are getting closer than we were yesterday. Be persistent in your endeavors, stay true to your beliefs, and do not let others deter you from the passion and determination you possess. Some may call me nuts, but hey, the mightiest majestic oak was once a nut who held its ground! Stay the path; have the will to endure no matter the obstacles! I myself have been knocked to the floor a hundred times, but you will see me stand right back up and hear me say, "Here comes one hundred and one." We all have the same vision, and that is to find answers. Always remember that every accomplishment over the course of history started with the decision to try. I choose to continue trying!

DARKNESS HAS A DOOR

T HERE WAS ONCE upon a time in a mysterious realm that a man searched for what seemed an eternity to find answers within. Day in and day out through the blackened shadows didst he seek. In the pitch-black darkness, he foraged forward through its murky and somber embrace. A still had fallen, a quiet like no other, as he felt it tighten its grip on his now-trembling soul. This very moment, coldness had become a resident here as if partner to all that is obscure and veiled in the shadows. He glances through the dark and beholds a glimmer, a welcoming illumination of beckoning light. "What is this which lies before me?" he asked himself. He reached out and made out the form of a key as he took it into his hand. Hereupon, he did determine that this key might be his answer to the messages and secrets that were hence locked within these darkened corridors. Feeling his way through the eerie and gloom-filled passage, he searched for the door that might lead him to the answers he so desperately yearned for. He thought to himself, "Time hath begun to pass heavily with me here in this darkness." Then it happened. A door before him, laden with iron and wood of years past, of times long ago! His very soul screamed to him, as if warning him of an impending danger. He wondered, "Will my quest for these answers finally end as they appear to me here, or doest the presence before me have malevolent and evil intention?" The decision made, he inserted the key and began to turn it slowly. The door creaked and resounded, as if echoing a haunting warning of a wretched evil waiting just behind it to devour all that dared enter. The man stood in dead silence as he saw, standing right there with breath whence from a foul and hideous place did come. Horror stricken, the man stood frozen, a permanent fixture in this cold black place. This, being a terror like none other the man had ever faced, caused him to jump backward and slam the door he had just opened. His trembling hands now searched for the keyhole so that he might lock this demon in the place from whence it came. Alas, the keyhole was no more; thus the portal could not be closed. What once was a glimmering key now took the form of a hideous spider with legs of barbs that did attempt to attach to the man's hand. "What madness is this?" cried out the horrified man. With flailing arms didst he try to egress this evil thing as it did crave his flesh and had want and desire to feed from him. At last, the malevolent and putrid form was released, and the man began to flee from this portal that led into darkness. He thought to himself, "What evil have I granted entry into thy realm, what blackness didst I awaken?" Then he was alarmed, and the longer he thought about it, the more his thoughts confused themselves, and all his knowledge and the sum of his courage were of no help to him at present. It seemed as if he ran for half a league as he neared his exit, where he would be free of this cruel entity that had manifested with evil intention. Flying through the door, he became relieved that this wretch of a thing was nothing now but a fading memory, never more to trouble him. As he lay down that night for a long-needed and welcoming slumber, he began to dream of this creature as it ate at his very mind. This lasted for a week plus a day, and he could endure it no longer, for now he noticed sores as they festered on his hand, and his back was tender from needlelike scratches unknown. Cold sweat had now taken hold, and unrelenting tremors had taken him and challenged his sanity. Standing in trepidation and unease, he realized that the evil and darkness he had hence laid invitation to just days past had chosen to host within him. And at length, that very day, he was lost, and at present, he was quite alone and desolate. Sadness and fear now were the occupants of his tormented heart. And heaviest his loss was his very soul now tarnished and spirit broken. Thus, in his pain, he knew that he could only lay blame upon himself, for it was he that opened a door so that evil could rear its ugly head. So beware ye weary travelers, for we never know when we too could follow this man's path and allow something demonic into our world because darkness doeth have a door, and with it open, there can be no happily ever after!

A Para Shoes

W E AS PARANORMAL investigators have pretty big shoes to fill. We walk in the footprints of those before us who have continued our search in times long ago. They faced ridicule and doubt in the days of yesteryear just as we do today, but they stood firm, they took a stand, and they held their ground. So the path they have laid out before us is but an imprint in time, which continues to lead us forward as we journey ahead in search of answers within the paranormal realm. We need to challenge ourselves each and every day to do just as well as our predecessors have in the past, and by doing so, we continue to build that bridge to knowledge and lay the foundation for others to follow in the future. Throughout the whispering breath of time, doubt has cast its veil over the eyes of those who may possess a want and desire to believe. With disconcertment, doubt has clasped its uncaring hands over the ears of those who need to listen and to understand. There are those of us that choose to continue and follow in these footprints, to stay the path that has been set before us throughout time. We have a vision to learn more about the existence of another realm no matter the obstacles we may face. Do not let the journey of those throughout the years be in vain. Learn from past experiences; gain knowledge from others both then and now. Yield not to those who will seek to belittle you. As I have always said in the past, our focus is vital, our determination is strong, our beliefs and diverse interactions drive us forward, and our passion in what we do will eventually lead us to the answers. So if you have been knocked to the ground, get the hell back up, wipe yourself off, and continue on the path. It's as simple as that!

TEAMWORK

AS PARANORMAL INVESTIGATORS, we must always remember just how important it is to function as a team and not as individuals. It is teamwork that will eventually lead us to success; it is teamwork that will build the strong foundation required for us to move forward. My loyalty lies with my teammates. I will stand up for them no matter what may come. If we are wrong and make mistakes, then we make them together; we do not lay blame on one individual. As I have stated in the past, we are all unique and diverse in nature. I embrace this and strongly believe that by doing so, there is no limit to what we can achieve. We must constantly adjust our ways to deal with change, challenges, and the conflicts we will face day to day in what we endeavor to achieve. By meeting the needs of the team, we are also responsible for meeting the needs of the individuals who are part of it. I have heard of some groups that have individuals who only show for an investigation yet never remain in contact during the course when nothing is happening. They do not assist in evidence review. They do not contribute their opinions. They do not attempt any contact until there is another investigation. Members such as this can bring down a team and, in my opinion, are in it for the wrong reasons, seeking only the thrill of the hunt. This in itself can cause devastation and division among the group members and thusly should be reacted on! We should exist as a bonded entity, a determined and focused group. As a team with diversities embraced, we must continue to radiate an unquenchable faith in what we can achieve, an insatiable thirst for knowledge, and a determined ideology that the possibilities are endless. Never settle for the results of other people. Know deep within yourself that there is more out there! And when your team falls under attack by the verbal atrocities that we all experience in our field by the arrogance of others, stand firm and remain focused as you continue your trek forward on a journey for knowledge. Always have the courage to follow your heart and trust your intuition. Embrace your team. Stand with them even in the most torrent of times. Adversity, you only make me stronger. Ridicule and the arrogance of others, you only make me laugh. Embracing my team and their diversities, this gives me hope! In order for us to succeed as teams in this field, we must first believe that we can! Build that alliance, strengthen your coalition, pull together, and work as one; by embracing these values, you will create an unwavering fellowship as you band together that no one person can bring you down!

New Paranormal Groups, We Got Your Back

A
HHHH, PARA-DRAMA, THE always-inevitable, assuming, and audacious actions of the hardcore skeptic! We have all had to deal with the arrogance of others in what we endeavor to achieve as paranormal investigators. Hell, none of us came into this field as all-knowing and have learned from our mistakes along the way. But even as a newly formed group, you must always stand firm, focused, and stay the path. Listen, I am my own worse skeptic, and I have learned from it and from my experiences. When we allow our fear of ridicule and rejection to affect how we determine to post what we may think to be evidence, it only hurts us in the end. It is my belief that no anomaly should go unnoticed, no matter how trivial it may be. There are those of us out there who will look at it from a respectful perspective and give our honest opinions based on our experiences we have incurred along the way. This is detrimental in the learning process, and if we let this para-drama affect our reasoning and determine how we conduct ourselves, we are only letting these self-proclaimed dictators of doubt win. Sure, they will have their little closed-minded lackeys jump on the bandwagon with them, but this is just a pitiful attempt at emoting some type of loudmouthed and narcissistic views they have created in their perfect little neverland! It is just an ego thing with them, and to tell the truth, it makes me laugh at times; thusly, I consider them free entertainment. Don't get me wrong; sometimes we may post something that is obviously not paranormal in nature, but we learn from it. Skeptics just cause us to look at ourselves and our evidence a little harder, which is a good thing. My advice to new groups is to not live in fear of ridicule, doubt, and rejection. Do not allow yourselves

to be pulled into this para-drama that exists among us today. Use your passion, keep your focus, and continue in your efforts! There are those of us that stand with you. Ignore the rants and raves of these egotistical self-proclaimed babbling idiots and do not, I repeat, *do not* let them drag you down to their level. What you do is important; what you do is vital. So I say again, stay the path. Learn from all of it, and you will be better in the end!

HAPPILY EVER AFTER-LIFE?

J UST WHAT IS our obsession with the afterlife? Afterlife, hereafter, next world, the other side, the spiritual realm—no matter what you may call it, we as a society seem to be obsessed with what will befall us once our time in this physical world is over and we pass on. Some believe that once we move on, our consciousness dies at the instance our brain ceases to exist. Others believe it continues to reside with us after we leave our physical shell here in this world. I mean, the possibility and actuality of losing an entire lifetime of emotion, life, consciousness, and memory seems devastating to us now. But do any of these elements actually remain with our souls in a life beyond? I mean, what facts and/or criteria do we apply as individuals to any general and rational reason as we endeavor to understand? I know that our different religious beliefs, individual values, and self-philosophies guide us to our own conclusions, but this in itself still leaves a perplexity that pulls me in various directions. As paranormal researchers, are we actually placing identity to lost souls, or are we just identifying their physical being as they lived among us in this realm? Is our traditional view of an afterlife just wishful thinking of what we want it to be only because we seek comfort in knowing that we will retain certain aspects of what we held dear here in the physical world? Will it be peaceful there? Is it lonely there? Is there really a happily ever after there? I, for one, want to know!

A LETTER FROM MY SOUL

MY DEAREST AND most beloved, I am here now in a place I cannot comprehend. It is dark and cold, and I am so alone. I yell out but am not heard. Shadows surround me and hold me in a tight embrace, denying me the warmth and the light. I miss you so much and find you in the thoughts of my soul and memory of my spirit. I remember my excited breath when I first laid eyes upon you. I feel so alone, so lost. Why am I in this place? I find my very spirit, my very soul missing you. I miss the times I would stare at you, mesmerized and in awe of your beauty, both in self and in heart. To touch you and kiss you at times would bring me to tears, though I would hide them. The whispers of "I love you" that were gently laid on each other's ears are now but a haunting memory. Each time our eyes would meet, I could see deep into your soul and feel a contentment and peace like no other. Memories of the heart and memories of the mind matter not, for they are now part of me here. Please know that I cherished your love and treasured all that we shared. I miss the soft and gentle touch of your hands. I miss the tender and warm embrace that only you could bestow on me. Time stood still when I was with you and my emotions stirred. If I only had that one last chance to hold you again, to show you how deeply I cherished you and loved you. You would see me shed that final tear as it streamed down my face and ended upon a smile that only you could pull from me. I would want to tell you that I loved everything about you and thank you for making all my dreams come true. You filled my world with love and warmth, and I hold this within my very soul and spirit for eternity. They say hope springs eternal; my hope in this empty place is for that to be true. Though I cannot bear the emptiness that comes from missing you, I will search for some light to lead me away from this blackness and on to that place where, one day, I will hold you in an eternal embrace. Until we meet again, feel me as I am missing you! Here is my point, maybe this is overexaggerated, but when we attempt contact with those that have passed, stop and think about what may be!

SILHOUETTE OF EVIL

W ITH RECENT EVENTS that have occurred in the world today, I am constantly reminded of the evil that exists in our society. There are those so dark and so evil that the only pleasure they can gain is by hurting others and destroying lives. What they do can crush the human spirit and sicken your very soul. I ask myself, what can make a person so corrupt, so harmful and uncaring toward others? No answer or reason comes to mind, only visions of the atrocities and havoc these depraved and repulsive animals have created. There is a sickness out there that walks among us each and every day, whose only intent is to hurt others and create devastation. Demonic by proxy, guilty by association with dark forces, chemical imbalances? Who knows the true reason that such hideous, vicious, and loathsome monstrosities can be allowed to exist in a world such as ours. The cold, hard fact is that they do, and the evil they reap upon us is devastating beyond all imagination. What's even worse is the fact that this brings out a dark side within myself I never knew existed. You know what I mean. Put me in a locked room with these depraved idiots with a padded golf club so that I may slowly beat them into unconsciousness over and over again and then send them on for their final judgment! I don't like seeing that side of myself as it truly saddens me. However, it's also at such times that people can discover their own inner resiliencies and strengths that can bring them together. It is when these horrifying images of devastation and heartbreak are indelibly etched in our collective consciousness that we come together as a caring and compassionate people. It is how we react in the face of crippling grief that will define us as human beings. We must maintain hope in the face of tragedy and strive for a better future for our children and for ourselves. We must not allow ourselves to be pulled down to the putrid and disgusting level that these sick demented few have created. We must look to help those that have been affected, whether it is in prayer or positive thought and action. In the face of adversity, we must remember that the true human spirit within each of us is good and empowered with a strength and resilience like no other. Those that have chosen the dark and evil path in life will find that it leads them to a hellish and well-deserved end. Remain strong and keep the hope alive! Do not allow yourself to fall under the looming shadow created by this silhouette of evil! We can make the difference!

LEGACY'S JOURNEY

A T A TIME when ancients still walked the earth and the time that is now was yet a speck not in sight of those who dwelled within such a place, there were those like ourselves destined to learn. In this faraway and magical land, there lived an old and withered soul of a king whose only wish was to learn and teach others of the secrets and wonders of a mystical realm from which the dead spoke in tongue and thusly wandered in search of light. But alas, in this land there also lived those that possessed eyes yet would not open them, had ears yet would not listen with them, and possessed all the senses gifted unto them but chose to let them lie in waste. They were known during these times as Skeptomanians, who worshipped the evil idol henceforth named as Skeptico in the barren, desolate lands of Skepticism. The king became saddened by such a people that would not change and open to a new light of learning and understanding. Thus, he proclaimed, "Bring to me two richly laden wagons filled with the knowledge gathered by all within our land, and we shall venture a journey into this black and dark land of Skepticism!" And so it came to pass that the trek forward was to be long and treacherous, but the dedicated people were determined and hence arrived at the gates of the city. "We have much to share among your people, we have much to teach and learn," declared the hopeful king. The arrogant people of Skepticism were of bad heart and became envious and jealous of the knowledge the king and his followers had since amassed. Attack was made upon the good people as dignities were stricken by harsh and cruel words; beliefs were pierced by the sharp blades of cold, blatant doubt and disrespect. But the king's determined and passionate followers stood strong and, on this day, were not fazed by this attack of stupidity and arrogance. While they conversed with one another, they contrived unknown to the dark ones that their light was not to be shared with this dark place never more. In jubilance, an echo was heard throughout the land as kings, princes, queens, councilors, knights, and the valiant people assembled and continued their journey to knowledge. Thereupon, the evil that dwelled in the land of Skepticism remained in the darkness, void of light, and from them sprang more of the sort. This did not matter to the king as he knew well that nothing shall deter them from that which they seek. They laid the path that was to be followed by others, and to this very day, our journey continues!

NOW, I LAY ME DOWN TO SLEEP

A HHHH, AT DAY'S end, we all look forward to that long-awaited, peaceful slumber as we wind down from the stresses and activities of our hectic day. But once we drift away in calming and solemn silence, our mind awakes and has orchestrated its very own production of beauty, happiness, sorrow, and sometimes, terrifying experiences to share. As Elias Canetti once stated, "All the things one has forgotten scream for help in dreams." No one can really say why we dream, but the belief exists that dreams may be our own mind's responses to events and actions that occur throughout the day. In some instances, they may even be a response to our conscience's most intimate wants and desires or even our darkest and horrific fears. Our dreams are unique to each and every one of us because it is our personal backgrounds, beliefs, emotions, and experiences that cause us to see and feel as only we can interpret these haunting images. I have dreamed all my life as I know most of us had. It is recently that my dreams have become more vivid and strange, and this, in itself, has caused me to try and understand more about why. Are they answers to questions that not even I can put into words or understand? Are they my mind's way of trying to make sense of or even attempting to show me a way to better understand? Or is it a possibility that someone or something is trying to communicate a message to me from a realm we do not fully comprehend in today's society? I believe that in our very spirit, our very soul, we are telling our own story when we dream. I also believe that contact from the other side most definitely can be made as we rest and become more open, less distracted. There are incredible and wondrous meanings to our dreams. Just what they are trying to tell me, I do not quite understand, but it mystifies me! I have decided to follow some of the hints and clues being shared with me in my dreams the past few days during my investigations. Hopefully, some things will become clearer, and I can add reason to their purpose.

AND WITH MALICIOUS INTENT

I N OUR INTEREST and even at times obsession with the paranormal, we lose sight of the risk we take each time we set out and conduct our research. Our want and our desire to find explanations for things that occur within the paranormal realm drive us with such a passion and determination that we sometimes lose sight that something dark and evil may be lying in wait for us. It is my belief that there is something demonic, call them what you like, which exists for the sole purpose of causing us ill and harm. Some that may provoke during an investigation may be opening themselves up to a physical attack or even a dark and malicious attachment. I believe in the existence of demons and that they possess intelligence well beyond ours. They can trouble and deceive our minds as they cause contention within our society as humans. The origins of the belief in demons among ancient societies have been shrouded in mystery for millennia and, to this very day, remain so. An attack by a demonic force may not be the case every time. I believe that an individual in life who lived as a bad and evil member of society will continue to do so in the afterlife and can wreak havoc on the living. No matter the case, we must remain vigilant in our purpose and take the necessary precautions! Whatever your religious or personal beliefs may be, there will always be something not of this realm that waits to drag you into its misery, into its torment. Do not open yourself to this type of contact as it is not only you that this beastly, corrupt, depraved, and damnable host will seek to destroy. It will attack those that you love and care about most and manipulate your lives to the point of devastating destruction.

This will always remain foremost in my mind as I continue my journey in search of answers—that lying in the shadows and concealed in blackness, there waits an evil filled with hate, with malice, and with malicious intent!

AN ILLUSION OF TRUTH?

WITH ALL THAT we endeavor in the field as paranormal investigators, there are certain truths that we must gather in order to put fact and proof of its reality to the test, thus adding legitimacy to what we find. We must begin to understand that there is so much more to the truth than just the known facts, so much more. With the existence of visual and even auditory pareidolia, or matrixing for a simpler term, we are constantly faced with an overwhelming realm of illusions. We then become fascinated by these so-called illusions in different ways by our perceptions alone. Not every one of us will respond to what our mind is registering in the exact same way. This does not mean that any of us are more intelligent than the other just based on the fact that we perceive it in a different way. So it should not upset you if an illusion of sorts is not as apparent to you as it is to those around you. Shadow figures, full-body apparitions, haunting mists and disturbing shapes, tormenting screams in the night, and the beckoning whispers of wandering spirits and souls. All of these are perceived differently by each and every one of us. I know that, for I myself believe they all do exist, but does this, in fact, affect how my own mind perceives these anomalies? Does my passion guide me away from viewing these activities as something that may be a typical and reasonable explanation and twist it to something mysterious and unknown? Am I really in full control of all my senses, or am I falling back on a predetermined analogy I have previously programmed myself for my own wants and desires? To answer all of these questions simply, I have to say no because I have grown here within the paranormal field and learned from my own misgivings and from others' experiences. I now view these mysteries with an open and skeptical mind, and I remain determined that by dissecting and analyzing these illusions, some will disappear while others will become proof of something wondrous within this spectacular realm. Losing the illusion makes us wiser than finding the actual truth, and we continue to grow from the experience! So are we really in control of how we perceive these occurrences? Has our decision been predetermined by our own mind-set? Are we simply guided by our inherent genes, our upbringing, a predetermined fate, a karma, or even our religious beliefs? Lose the illusion and gain the truth and knowledge that will remain. Or is that, in itself, an illusion of truth?

IN THIS THE FINAL RESTING PLACE

WHILE REVELING IN the images of death and the horrors of the grave, one can only cast perceptions of haunting, dark, and sorrowful meaning as we apply these images to the place we are laid to rest at life's end. Yet there is a haunting and calming beauty if we only look deep within. With flowers laid and majestic trees casting their restful shade over these hallowed grounds, one cannot help but feel and see the emotions that have become a permanent part of this serene and silent place. The whispering winds caress this sacred ground with an almost mournful cadence as it travels effortlessly over these beds of earth, now host to the physical shell of lives passed. There is a certain artistry that embraces your very spirit here, both in heart and in mind. Does spirit and soul wander these grounds? Do the angels stand sentry and sing a melodious lullaby as if to bless what is now a dreamless final rest for the occupants within? Headstones mark each site inscribed with note and verse of love and memories past in an elegance of sorrow and sometimes humorous yet loving jab. Though this is a sad and silent place, there is an enchantment that embraces you with the grace that dwells within its gated walls. Harmonious in its own way, a story can be heard here, a tale of times past and wonders of times still to come. Looking at and understanding the picturesque and resplendent beauty here brings a solemn feeling to one's very soul and spirit. So the next time you pass these restful grounds, reflect on them a while as the warm, soft scent of spring grass and the comforting cool breeze of calm awakens you. As the memories flash before you, as the desolation grasps at your emotions, as its artistry is shared with you like a masterpiece in time, take the time to feel and see the true and hidden beauty that does exist here in this final resting place!

WITHOUT THEM

FOUNDING A PARANORMAL group and conducting research in itself does not make us effective leaders by any means. A good leader is one not born but someone created within themselves and by others around them. We must possess the desire, willpower, determination, and passion to embrace others on our teams along with their diversities in order to grow. It is vital that we inspire our team members and nurture their beliefs, opinions, views, and ideas if our goal is to be effective leaders. We need to constantly strive and continually work to improve our leadership skills. Never rest on your laurels! I cannot stress this enough: it is our team members, not us, that will determine whether or not we are successful as leaders in the paranormal field. If we lose their trust and confidence, they will become uninspired, and without them, we are basically nothing. With the type of work that we do, it is vital that we constantly inspire a shared vision with our team, enable them to act, model the way by showing that we can achieve success. Don't be the boss who dictates to others what to do; be the leader who meets the challenges alongside with their teams! We must always and, most importantly, encourage the hearts of our teams by sharing the glory with our members and embracing their diversities. By doing this, we empower them, and by capitalizing on all their strengths and differences, we are able to meld as one, a most powerful and unwavering force in our field of study. We must show understanding and compassion and embrace their diversities because when we ignore them, we become nothing more than arrogant dictators. Listen to their ideas, hear their thoughts and beliefs, consider their ideas and values. Do all of these and you are on your way to being that effective leader. Holier-than-thou arrogance, that's not who we are; there are many people that will walk into and leave our lives, but it is truly our team members that will define us and leave their unique footprints in our minds and in our hearts. Without them, we are nothing!

VOICES

ISEMBODIED AND HEARD in the moment or caught as an EVP, as paranormal investigators, we are dedicated to understanding and trying to apply some reason to these messages we receive from the other side. No matter the means of its delivery, we need to realize that at this very moment, two souls are meeting as one voice, and the captivating message we receive is an attempt to lead us to something. Sure, there are times when a message is heard that is more than likely an imprint in time, but on that same note, there are times when someone from the other side is attempting to send us a message, to contact us from beyond. At times, they are warnings of an impending danger. Then at other times, it seems as though these souls are reaching out for someone to guide them or even to find a caring ear to share their lonesome tales of woe. Though it resembles distant memories fading in and out, there is a powerful and emotional message waiting to fall on a willing ear, an open mind, and a caring soul. Voices have been calling out for an eternity, and it is our responsibility to listen to them and try and make sense of the intended message and not revel in the thrill of the capture alone. We need to understand that once a soul/spirit has moved on, it has been isolated from a world it once knew, it has left happiness behind, and heavy sorrow now embraces it. Now trapped and lost in darkness, dreams snuffed by the shadows, they call out for anyone to just listen to their message. Whether it is to us or just a result of the torment they may be suffering, we need to try and understand their soul shared message. I take their words to heart as my mind and soul replays them constantly, and I attempt to add sense and reason to them. Whispers in the night, echoes sung from the shadows, screams of terror and rage that pierce our very souls, these are all an attempt to send us a message, and it is up to us to try and understand and hear their meaning as we are audience to their voices!

In The Eyes Of The Beholder

I N MY EXPERIENCES as a paranormal investigator, I have worked with individuals who generally developed preconceived notions prior to an investigation. I have probably been guilty of it myself a time or two, but I have come to the realization that it can only hurt us in the end as far as our research is concerned. There have been times in the past when I worked with a group who, after initial client interview, would make the determination that this individual is loony or some sort of nutcase. In the end, our purpose is damaged because of the attitude we enter our investigation with or just decide not to continue. Don't get me wrong, there will be cases out there that we know for sure are not legitimate, but it is not our right to judge clients on this merit alone. Our preconceived notions can cast a looming shadow that then conceals even more of that which we attempt to seek and learn from. Think of it this way: a young child just beginning to learn to walk has no preconceived notion that they cannot succeed on the first few attempts. Imagine what would happen if we said, "Don't try to walk, you will fail." Doesn't make sense, does it? As paranormal researchers, we often send ourselves failure messages due to our preconceived notions and do not take advantage of opportunities because we are afraid we will not succeed or they are not worth our time and effort. Is it our conscious or unconscious conditioning that we have been subjected to our entire life that leads us to this type of behavior? We need to remain determined and resilient and not let any opportunity pass, no matter how trivial we may think it is. If we continue on a path with these negative preconceived notions, we can only look forward to conditioning others to not even attempt new things that could eventually lead to answers. It is how we view the final outcome, it is how we see the possibilities of wonder and mystery that will open our minds and our eyes. Treat every opportunity as brand-new, approach it as something you have never tried, never heard, never done, never judged, and most importantly, never had a preconceived notion toward. In the eyes of this beholder, it is not just what we know how to do right now in this instant that counts but what we can do each and every day and the endless possibilities that do exist! And that is looking through the eyes of this beholder!

MIND FORECAST, PARTLY CLOUDY TO SUNNY

T HE POWER OF the mind and the possibilities within it has always fascinated me. Our minds hold the key to our spiritual growth, our self-growth, and to opening doors we never imagined existed before. The secret is concentrating, visualizing, seeing details, having faith, and projecting emotionally. When your mind is empty from thoughts and worries and only one single thought is allowed to enter, it gains a great and infinite power. In our daily lives, we are hindered by predominant thoughts and habits that, in turn, cloud our judgments and our ability to completely open ourselves to new horizons or trying new things. I myself create a mind-set prior to any investigation where I clear my mind of all that has occurred throughout the day and in my life—a sort of cleansing, you might say. This calms the mind and opens it to the wondrous possibilities that then can begin to interact with it. We have to train ourselves until it turns into second nature and it becomes easier to obtain this state of calm. It's a lot like being outside on a bright, sunny day. Sure, the clouds may move in and completely cloak the radiance and comforting warmth of the sun, but beyond the clouds remains the sun in all its glory! We need only to clear the clouds of thought that envelop our own minds and open it up to whatever may be waiting to interact with it. Our thoughts, ideas, habits, and beliefs constantly occupy our minds, which can deter us from focusing on and understanding what is happening around us. Your mind is a wondrous and powerful thing. Utilize it fully. The possibilities and hidden secrets of this realm are waiting for you to clear a place for it so that it may share with you!

TEAM SUPPORT, IT GOES BOTH WAYS!

WHEN DEALING WITH our paranormal teams as founders, cofounders, or even team leads, it is vital that we support our teams 100 percent, no matter what the case may be. We know that it is through their diverse beliefs and constant efforts that we will succeed. But on the other side of the coin, we must also have the support of our team members in all our endeavors. A leader is typically responsible for setting a base agenda, facilitating information, and monitoring progress by communicating with members as needed. But all actions must be agreed upon by all involved. You may have the best idea, but not everyone may understand it the first time. The same question may be asked more than once. A member may forget a deadline unless reminded. Disagreements may occur over small details. Communication and participation are vital within the team. There are times that we must stop and reevaluate our members and the support they are willing to dedicate to what we are trying to achieve. A team is defined as a group (a collection of people) who interact to achieve a common goal, but an effective and well-functioning team is much more than this. The interaction in the beginning may have been most impressive. But after some time has passed, you wonder why team member involvement slacks off, and the only interactions you receive are when you are presented with a case or location that makes all others seem like small potatoes and even then may be ignored. Participants in an effective team care about the group's well-being. They skillfully combine appropriate individual talents with a positive team spirit to achieve results. So we need to ask ourselves, do your members believe in the value of working together in a team effort? Do your members believe that a team decision or product can be superior to the work of a single individual? Has your team made a personal commitment to work with one another in a team effort? Has the collection of individuals made a commitment to work together in a team? These are important issues and vital to our cause. If their dynamics have changed and you begin to realize that the only thing they care about is the status of being in a paranormal group and the popularity it may bring, well it's time to reevaluate your processes for the good of the team and what you're striving to achieve. It's important to realize that the development of effective working relationships among team members is a gradual process that requires considerable time and skill. Supporting your team is vital and necessary, but at the same time, we need their support.

WHEN I AM GONE

WHEN MY TIME here upon this earth has faded and I take my last struggling breath, when I have cleansed my tired eyes one final time with my departing and sorrow-filled tears, when I slip quietly away into that final and long-awaited eternal slumber, when I cease to exist in this physical realm and, by chance, end up lost in the spiritual world, do not come in search of me without care and compassion in your hearts, without a mutual respect, and approach me with provocation. Lost souls, no matter what path they may have followed in their physical life, deserve our respect and compassion as every human being does! Do not approach me with intent to provoke only because you believe it will bring you an astonishing result that you can brag about and share with others. You, my friend, did not walk in my shoes. You did not live as I once did. I laughed with my family, I loved those dearest to me, I wept in times of sorrow, I cared for others, I felt sadness, happiness, heartbreak, loneliness, and I walked this earth once just as you do today. It is my belief that I will still hold true to my feelings and emotions once it has been determined my time has ended here, even though I am free of my physical body. Come to me with provocation, and I will feel nothing but sadness and sorrow for you. I will then ask you; why does a human being do something so uncaring as this? We must, and I wholeheartedly emphasize, *must* show care, compassion, and respect when dealing with someone who has passed on to the spiritual world, and those that do not will not earn my respect. What we do as paranormal investigators is not a joke; it is not an excuse for seeking some self-gratifying thrill and afterward moving on. Remain professional in your cause. Show the morality each of us possesses deep within us and show the respect that each and every one of us deserves, whether it be here and now or "when I am gone"!

THE CALMING BEAUTY BECKONS ME

WHILE VISITING DIFFERENT areas during my travels, I love to stop in and see towns no longer occupied by human inhabitants. If you stop and really look at them for a short moment, you can see and hear a presence as it tries to beckon to you with its silent and calming beauty. Each year, I set out on a journey along roads not often traveled. I find towns no longer occupied by life and song. As I visit these so-called ghost towns, I see and feel the hustle and bustle of what once filled these desolate sagebrush-and-dust-covered streets. The memories of life here have not been erased and forgotten; they are just waiting for someone to feel, to understand, and to relive their history. The silence here is like music; the continuous clouds draw you into a peaceful calm as inspiration settles in, takes you by the hand, and begins to add you to the chapters of the story being told here in this very spot as it has been told for an eternity. The wind itself plays out a certain harmony as it whips and dances through the buildings, walkways, and trees that still stand majestically in its memory. This sends your mind into a trancelike state as you begin to imagine. Imagine what it must have been like to be a part of this wondrous and beautiful place once upon a time long past. Imagine the life this desolate and forgotten town was once host to. Imagine the stories that have been carved into its landscape and monumental buildings, which now stand empty. Imagine all of this and you will see that this place is not dead at all. It is very much alive, and as you walk in the footsteps it has laid before you through its peaceful and inviting calm, you will feel its beauty, you will feel its history, you will feel and hear its story as you feel it beckoning you!

KUDOS TO THE SKEPTIC

S KEPTICISM HAS MANY definitions but generally refers to any questioning attitude of knowledge, facts, or opinions/beliefs stated as facts, or doubt regarding claims that are taken for granted elsewhere. Personally, I respect the skeptic for all that they do and welcome their criticism in our paranormal studies. I mean, if it were not for skeptics, we would take everything that is said as the given word, and where would we be then? The need for clear and concise scientific proof and reasoning, which they are so famous for, is not asking all that much as far as I am concerned. Listen, we as paranormal investigators are the same way and should always be our most critical skeptic. I understand that there are hardcore skeptics out there that no amount of proof will ever convince, but the dose of skepticism we receive in paranormal research should only prove to keep us on our toes. I believe that when we die, our spirit survives and can sometimes communicate with the living. I also believe in ESP, astral projection, angels, demons, and just about anything that may exist in the spiritual realm. Some of my beliefs have a legitimate basis of evidence to support it, and some do not, meaning they are only beliefs and have no scientific basis whatsoever. Hear me when I say I doubt, I require hard proof, I need to review every possible avenue of scientific evidence before I will believe anything to be paranormal in nature. So thusly, I am a skeptic, not a novice skeptic, but a full-blown, five-alarm, what-the-hell-was-that skeptic! Thusly, I say with truth, kudos to the skeptic!

CAUSE TO DREAM

A dream is a work of art which requires of the dreamer no particular talent, special training, or technical competence. Dreaming is a creative enterprise in which all may and most do participate.

—Clark S. Hall

HAVE YOU EVER wondered why you dream? This question has fascinated people since the beginning of recorded history, but today we still don't fully understand the purpose of our dreams. Is it a form of psychotherapy we develop during our lifetime? Is it just a representation of our unconscious desires and wishes? Or is it maybe just the way our brain consolidates and processes information we take in on a daily basis as we sleep? I know I often find myself wondering, why the—did I just dream that! As our memories seem to intensify during the dreaming stage, most people forget 95 percent of all dreams immediately upon their awakening. I have discovered that since I became interested in the paranormal, I tend to remember my dreams in great detail and almost always. I wonder if in any way the study and interactions with the paranormal and all that relates to it have aided in opening a portion of our minds to the point where we can recollect more from our dreams. Could it also be that we dream more vividly about impossible things, dark things, and remarkable things, all because of our interests and/or contacts within the paranormal realm? Or is it due to another influence such as something dark and malevolent from the spirit realm that has found a new place to dwell? In our minds and in our dreams!

HEAVEN AND HELL

(This beginning statement is not specifically my belief.)

"THE BIBLE IS considered to be a reasonable book. There is nothing at all that is viewed as contradictory about it: everything fits together in a manner that makes its message both dynamic and easy to understand, with absolutely no doubts. Its teachings make an undeniable sense and it is this simple logic that presents such a challenge that not one person of good can deny its impact."

The immortal soul is variously described as a "never-dying entity," a "divine spark," and to it are attributed all the characteristics of what is termed the real man—personality, conscience, reason and understanding, emotions, and all the moral qualities of which man is capable. The body is said to be mortal and corruptible, turning to dust and ashes after death, whereas the soul is immortal and incorruptible and lives on in endless bliss or misery. The existence of a heaven or a hell is a very controversial subject, and in our dealings with the paranormal, I am quite interested in the thoughts of everyone out there as to their beliefs of the existence of these two places. And as paranormal researchers, do our beliefs have anything to do with how we view our investigative tactics? There are so many interpretations existing on different areas of the Bible. Your religious beliefs and what you have been taught determine how you interpret it. I see that most religions believe a majority of the writings and agree with the same outlooks, but there still remain areas that certain religions interpret the meanings completely opposite. Do we as paranormal researchers let our religious beliefs and interpretations of these writings determine how we initiate are studies? Just curious!

Reality Check Human Research Group (RHRG)

HELLO, I AM known as Shadow here in the spiritual realm, founder of RHRG. You could consider me a ghostwriter of sorts! Some of my "soul" mates and I have developed this group to study the existence of humans and the way they interact with the spirit world. During our HVP (human voice phenomenon) sessions, we ask very specific questions. The following are some of them.

1. Why do you come here and shout profanities at us?
2. Why do you show disrespect toward us?
3. Why do you present items of violence that have been part of our demise?
4. Why do you desecrate our final resting place?
5. Why do you not show one iota of care or pity when searching for us?
6. Why is it that your heart is so cold and morality is but a stranger to your being?

We have captured so much overwhelming and indisputable evidence that has even turned our most critical skeptics into truly heartfelt believers! I now know why our three-clawed companions here like to take a swipe at some of you on occasion. So after reviewing our evidence in observing some of the humans we interact with, we have come to the undisputed and inarguable conclusion, along with our undeniable evidence, that "assholes" really do exist! On behalf of me and my team, we hope that you do not become one of our file inputs and that evidence captures such as this will decline in the future as we are running out of storage space for it. Thank you for listening!

SOUL TO SOUL

THE OTHER DAY, we spoke of the human soul and the possibility of its existence with emotional binding in a spiritual world. As I reflected more on this, I remembered an important and vital aspect of the human soul and how we interact with it during our investigations. As we initiate our electronic voice phenomenon (EVP) sessions, do we really stop and think of the method used when we are speaking? By this, I mean, we are trying to contact a lost and lonely soul, dwelling in the darkness, absent of light, cold and lost in the unrelenting blackness of a realm not fully understood. So when I ask wandering spirits a question of this kind, I ask from deep into my own soul. I ask with compassion, I ask with care, and I ask with the true emotion that exists deep within myself. You could say that I want to communicate "soul to soul." Others who just ask a basic and sometimes disrespectful question and are doing it just to receive a recording they can just throw out there and to me are just not doing it for the right reasons. The emotions of love, warmth, caring, sadness, sorrow, sharing, and morality, I believe wholeheartedly, are bound with the soul and, thus, everlasting. If you have a true and caring soul, ask your questions directly from it, and let it lead you to the answers you search. A direct link from your very own soul to these poor and lost souls may bring you better results and possibly make you feel better about the way you approach paranormal research. It all falls back to showing the respect that these lost and wandering souls deserve. So when you dial in and want to communicate with them, use the "soul to soul" network and speak with care and compassion.

REFLECTIONS OF SILENCE

A S I SIT in the blinding darkness of night during an investigation, I take the time to reflect in reverence of the silence that surrounds and embraces me. I wonder, is this a time when my very own soul communicates with whatever souls may exist here in the blackness of night? Silence is much like a calming and tempting shadow that invites us to leap with our own souls into its beckoning and awaiting depths. Though it seems dark and mysterious at times, through our heart and soul, we can both hear and see more clearly the story that is about to unfold before us. Once you become aware of the silence and what it holds within its walls, you become more open to what it has to say. Listen for the lost souls as they cry out for the compassion of another caring soul. There are dark souls and there are kind souls that endure in the silence, so take the time to listen to them. You will begin to see that what was once elusive and deceptive in the night will start to come into the light. You will see that within yourself, there is wisdom to be gained through humility and knowledge to be gained through listening with your heart. Then and only then will you begin to hear the silence. You will see that within silence things can grow, souls can live, and the glimmer of moonlight can help light your path to hearing. Silence will take hold of your soul and guide you to hear its own melody as it becomes part of the orchestrated story just waiting to be shared. Everything we know exists in silence, as if silence itself is a renewing and revitalizing sleep of the soul itself. I respect silence, I listen to silence, and I learn from silence. Take the time to sit back and reflect in the silence and be ready for the story it has to share with you!

HE HARDEST THING

AS PARANORMAL RESEARCHERS, one of the hardest things we have to deal with is the spirit of what could be a lost sweet and innocent child. If you are an investigator possessing the heart and compassion I believe is required for our jobs, you will feel the pain and torment of this young and frightened innocence. A small child that cries out in the darkness as if feeling so alone, so cold and afraid, lost without anyone to hold them and console their tiny souls truly wrenches at my heart. Each time I hear a child in the shadows, I know at that moment a story is being told. Do their tiny little souls feel abandoned as if someone has left them behind? Do they feel that no one longer cares for them? Do they feel as if they are lost and nobody is trying to find them or listen to them anymore? Are they wondering if this is all just a bad dream or maybe they hold that tiny bit of hope that someone caring and loving is coming to save them, coming to guide them into the light and warmth they once held dear? As an investigator, it tears directly into my very own soul to imagine that this may very well be the case. That is one of the most important reasons I do what I do. I have the compassion to feel for others lost in darkness. I have the willingness to try and help in any way I can. I see their misery, I feel their hurt, I sense their fear, and I hear their tiny little cries in the night. I only wish I could reach out my arms to them, embrace them, and share with them the warmth that is now absent from their tiny little souls. I will continue to reach out for the children that are lost and wandering in this unknown realm. When I cease to feel this way and no longer care about this the way that I do now, it will be my time to move on into this dimension plagued with mystery and dark, hidden secrets, and even then, I will reach out to them. Dealing with an innocent child crying out in the blackness will always be to me the hardest thing!

ANTIPARASITICPERSEVERANCE

D ON'T WASTE YOUR time looking this up in *Webster's*; it's not there. It's just a blast making up big words to help make my point! It is true that people throw rocks at things that shine. You may notice that, on occasion, there are those who come out of the woodwork for no other reason but to ridicule and launch harsh comments of doubt directly at the progress you are making and the goals you are trying to achieve. I can take the skepticism to a point, but only when it is valid. As for those who make a habit of feeding off others who are trying to make a difference, I just write them off as arrogant parasites and continue on with what I do. Taking that first step as we have done is not enough. We need to continue the path to the end, so I consider these minor distractions just that—minor! For us to accomplish our goals, we need to laugh off these parasites and feel nothing but pity for them. Eventually, they will move on to another more vulnerable host until they begin feeding on one another. We have a powerful ability within us. It is the ability to control or reject unnecessary or harmful impulses that attempt to affect us. It is the ability to arrive at a decision and follow it with perseverance until its successful accomplishment. We need to disregard and reject doubts and thoughts about failure that others attempt to force upon us. Visualize your goals and stay the path. Don't let others be the obstacles that deter you from achieving success. So be confident and have faith in yourself and what you are doing. Perseverance will help you obtain that which you seek on your journey into the paranormal!

U-NIGHT WITH ME

MAYBE YOU THOUGHT I misspelled "unite" on this one. I think not! Just another crazy spelling to get a point across. Though most people may fear the night, I embrace it. When all the wonders of daylight are cloaked and hidden in the darkness, I look to the things that choose to reveal themselves in the night. We become more open to both the physical and the spiritual realm once the calm of night befalls us. I seek out my companions in the night, and on the guest list, I see the secrets, the dreams, the fantasies, the wonders, and the stories of souls around each and every turn. I feel my own soul's curiosity, enthusiasm, intensity, and ambitions as my desires begin to come to life. With compassion, I am able to open up both my mind and soul and walk in the footsteps of those that once filled this place with their joys and their struggles. As souls wander through this night, I do not fear to blindly follow them through the seeming chaos set out before me. At times, I may mourn their misery and loneliness, but I remain focused on the very thought of maybe being able to help, even if it's just by sitting and listening to their story. When you think about it, what we do here is a journey; it can lead us to unimaginable wonders that exist here and now and have existed for a millennium. As long as we choose to learn from this journey and face it and all the adversity that accompanies it, we will find that we can be proud of what we do and seek to achieve. Do not let anyone tell you that what you do is crazy or really doesn't make a difference. I for one can tell you that you do matter and what you strive to achieve will eventually materialize before you! So look inside yourself, trust your inner voice, gather that strength that will guide you along this path, and believe in the passion that now exists within your very own soul! No one can take this from us—no one! So *u-night* with me in this continuous effort. You are not alone!

THE TEACHING TREE

DRIVING TO WORK before dawn one morning, I noticed a tree as it stood alone in a field reflecting the light of the moon as it danced among its swaying branches. I reflected on it for a while and tried to relate it to us as paranormal groups and how we develop much like the tree. Have you ever really looked at a tree and thought about all that it endures yet remains a structured force in this unstable and changing world? I mean, look at all that it accomplishes, providing life, resources, shelter, and beauty. I think about when we have passed on and we become nothing but dust within the earth; they will remain, standing as strong as ever. As paranormal groups, we need to develop our strongly rooted foundation also so that we may stand strong against the winds of adversity. The lone tree gives us so much; it is our bed upon birth, our shelter in life, and our final resting place when our time is complete in this realm. Even then, the majestic tree will wave its mournful arms above the graves set out for our final sleep. They are beautiful in their peacefulness and so very wise as they stand in their wondrous silence. They grow and pass in life, just as we do, but during their lifetime, they stand tall, proud, and resilient against all odds. We should do the same as we all develop together. Let's build that foundation with powerful roots and nurture it with the wisdom we share among one another. Even though the doubtful winds of change and adversity will continue to torment and threaten us, we will remain a permanent force to be reckoned with as we stand as one. Even though the torrent winds may scatter our leaves upon the ground on occasion, we will know that they shall return, brighter and stronger each time as we learn from it. So to the lonely tree I see, standing as one in the field, I say thank you. Thank you for all that you do for us in life. You can now add "teacher" to your résumé as I have now learned from you!

JUST A LITTLE PASSION

WITHIN SILENCE, THERE exists a certain unspoken beauty, and when we pay attention, we learn from it. There is no substitute for what we can learn from the beauty that lies within this peaceful waiting silence. There is a creative inspiration, and there is knowledge just waiting to be shared. Whether you are inside a majestic and historical structure or outside enjoying the wonders of nature, both can bring to you its own sweet rewards. It's not up to us to bring the beauty into existence; we don't even have to work at it. All that is required from us is just knowing that beauty in silence is there and begin to listen to it and see it. Only then will we learn to appreciate it. Compose yourself and lock into the mind-set that allows the compelling beauty to lure you into its inviting embrace. It is like a solemn emptiness has been left behind for some special reason, maybe for us to feel and experience it as a passed soul may have wanted. Open yourself to the beauty of silence, and you will stand in awe at the story that may soon befall you as you begin to share and become a part of the story and the empty void that lay in wait for someone to listen, someone to care. As you are ushered into the performance before you, respect it and begin to learn from it. Like the stars above that have shone their brilliance for an eternity onto the murkiest of nights, spirits and wandering souls have also existed, and I believe they want to share their brilliance also. Though it may seem creepy, cold, and dark sometimes, take a moment to stop and see the beauty of silence or even connect with it and the mysteries within that have long been lost. What was once elusive and hidden from you may become brilliantly clear with just a little passion for the beauty of silence!

DISCOURAGED?

I'M NOT PROUD of it by any means, but there are times when I get discouraged by others. Most of us believe in the existence of a world occupied by spirits, lost souls, dark and lurking shadows, and unspoken and hidden secrets. But just how far does that really get us as legitimate paranormal investigators? I'm sure you've seen many documentary programs on television that tend to sensationalize the paranormal and give us all a bad name and impede what we are trying to achieve. You know the ones I'm talking about. A particular house or castle is investigated because it is said to be haunted and loaded with activity. Most of us have seen the so-called spirit orbs/dust floating across the screen, mediums supposedly being taken over by dark and haunting spirits, unexplained noises off in the distance, doors opening or closing by themselves, and EVPs being recorded and played back for our entertainment. Some of it is quite convincing, and some may even be true, but the very fact that none of it is taken seriously by the scientific community and today's society means that all of it continues to remain lost in translation because of the false premises used to produce such a circus! So we, as serious paranormal researchers, are back to faith versus fact. I myself hold true and certain this one belief—just because something has not been scientifically proven to be a fact does not mean it is considered to be false. Many times, people lose sight of this and assume everything is false unless proven 100 percent scientifically to be true. My personal opinion is that when it comes to matters of my faith, of my values, and of my own beliefs, I seek wholeheartedly to prove it to no one but myself. I am secure with my own conclusions and will not attempt to force them on others. I only seek to share what I have found. Whatever opinion you choose to form is completely up to you; however, it will not affect mine!

PARANORMAL CONTENTMENT

W E MAY NOT regard the paranormal world solely from the standpoint of our own prosperity, our own fulfillment, or even our own inner contentment. So many people exist in the world today. There are those, such as us, who were born to help others and strive to learn from one another and better ourselves. And there are those who stray from the path we follow and try to pull us into a stagnant zone of uncertainty with them. There are so many unknowns in the paranormal world today, so much we are unsure of. Many individuals throughout history have set out to discover new things, gather more knowledge, and unmask the mysteries in life to better our society. Look at where we would be today if they had not taken that first step on their journey to discovering the truth and creating a better understanding for all humankind. As we continue down that very same path as paranormal investigators, we bear the responsibility of remaining focused and dedicated for the very same cause. We need to share with one another and learn from one another. Though we may feel as if we are taking a beating or running into brick walls on a regular basis, all we need is to stand firm in what we believe and what we are trying to achieve. Given, the spiritual realm is dark and riddled with hidden secrets and laden with unknowns but full of new possibilities. Let's take everything we have learned in the past, combine it with what we are learning now, and set a goal to use it all to our benefit in the future to try and achieve a better understanding of the answers that have been cloaked for millennium in the shadows. We are the generation to lead; we set now the guidelines and the footprints on a pathway for future researchers to follow and continue our journey. I am not a timid soul by any means; I will not be discouraged by failures or setbacks. Doubt me if you like, but whether I achieve or fail in my purpose, I will know that I have tried, and knowing that will fill me with a contentment and pride unimaginable.

It's A Better View From Up Here

HARDSHIPS, LIKE MOUNTAINS, can seem almost impassable and even overwhelming at times. They try to communicate to us that they have been around much longer than us, and we can't do anything about them as they stand before us, blocking our way and clouding our view. And like mountains, they can seem intimidating. But we must not allow any difficulty, obstacle, or hardship to intimidate us as paranormal investigators. We will face these hardships on a daily basis, but if we focus our sights far above into the sunshine, we will see and discover our highest aspirations. Choose to soar above the clouds, race through the storms, and discover the light that dwells there, which will allow you to view all that is now hidden and confined by your mountains of hardship. Encountering mountains or difficulties in life is inevitable. We all will come across them. It is how we view these obstacles and deal with them that will determine our final outcome. So when I am faced with my mountains/hardships/obstacles, I choose to take flight and soar well above them. Believe me, it is a much better view from up here! Stay the path and savor the journey. There is something magical just waiting for you to find it!

DEMONS AMONG US

FROM PERSONAL EXPERIENCE, I can truly say that demons do exist among us, whether it is our own personal demons we face day to day or the dark and vile creatures that exist in the shadows that try to draw us in. Demons were once angels designed and created by God for a purpose. Those angels were created in what we call a hierarchy. They were created with various levels of intelligence and purpose. They were created with commanders and underlings of various calibers. The highest orders of angels known to humankind are called archangels. These are the most intelligent and powerful angels in all of creation. These angels are only sent to worlds that have life on them, worlds like Earth. Their knowledge of creation is unfathomable. Their power comes from that knowledge as well as the legions of angels they command. Even though demons are thought to possess a physical body, it is important that we remember they were once angels and they have spiritual abilities. Meaning, they do not need to be present in order to affect, control, or afflict someone. They send their underlings, minions, or shadowy entities to do their bidding for them. There are many legions that exist in the underworld/hell. As we investigate the paranormal realm in today's world, we need to remain aware of the fact that these dark entities are there and would love nothing more than to attach to us and destroy us personally and all that we hold dear. So please do not intimidate, do not challenge, and do not make a game of these dark forces. They can attach to you and manipulate you both physically and mentally and, additionally, torment the ones you love and care about. Believe me, you do not want these vile creatures as houseguests! Our research is important. It is vital. There are so many unanswered questions that exist in the spiritual realm, but we must always—and I mean always—be aware that there are demons among us!

PERCEPTIONS PERCEIVED

BASING DECISIONS ON our own perceptions is what drives us to the conclusions that we hold to be true or actual reality. How we perceive things in the paranormal field depends really on what we are actually in search of. In today's society, there are those who choose not to accept certain events that occur in the paranormal realm judged only on their own opinion. No matter how valid our evidence may seem, there will always be someone standing by ready to tell you that you are wrong based only on their opinion. It takes a considerable amount of courage to do what we do and to lay ourselves out there for others to ridicule. There is really no way around it, and it remains a fact of life we must deal with constantly. We cannot let the perceptions of others who remain closed-minded to deter us in what we are trying to achieve—answers and reason. If we are to make any difference at all in proving that the paranormal does exist, we must dare to push forward and not be derailed by others. In unity we stand as one, we stand as a strong and unrelenting force! We owe it to ourselves, and to others, to remain focused and not be drawn in by the perceptions of others arrogant enough to believe their way is the only way! So no matter how crazy or unbelievable your evidence may be, share it with others. There are those of us that do believe in the mysteries and possibilities that remain hidden from view. We use our perceptions in a positive and open-minded way as we try and understand. We have embarked on a journey into the unknown, but we have taken that first step together, and it is together that we can all make the difference. At least, that's how I perceive it!

SOUL EVERLASTING

THE SOUL, EASY to define but almost impossible to explain, is basically defined as the animating and vital principle in humans, credited with the faculties of thought, action, and emotion and often conceived as an immaterial entity. The spiritual nature of humans, regarded as immortal, separable from the body at death, and susceptible to happiness or misery in a future state. Or even the disembodied spirit of a dead human. In Christianity, the soul is all-important. However, because the Bible does not give a formal definition of the concept, Christian interpretations vary greatly. At death, the soul withdraws and continues to function in the spiritual world. So I ask myself, do these souls merely move on to a predestined area, or can they possibly become lost in searching for a path into the light? I know that with myself, I feel love for others deep into my soul; my emotions are held warm deep into my soul, and all that are considered dear and close to me remain as strength to my soul. So when my physical shell is done on this earth, it is my belief that my soul will retain these emotions, and as I loved and cared for you once, I shall continue to love and watch over you for an eternity. People everywhere are searching for well-being, for meaning in their lives, to feel a purpose, to obtain fulfillment, health, and happiness. For life to be good, we need to feel useful and appreciated, and once we pass on, I believe this will accompany us. This is where my main point comes across. Knowing that this is a distinct possibility, paranormal researchers should hold on to this belief as they continue in their research. We are not trying to communicate with some animated character that we have created in our own uncaring minds. We are trying to speak with souls that may be lost but still hold these emotions deep within. Why anyone would disrespect this in any way or manner totally escapes me. When we can finally learn to understand, show love and respond to a soul as if it were ours, lost in the darkness and in search of something pure and calming in the light, we will then find meaning and be proud of what we may have accomplished. Do not bully these poor lost souls with provocation. Talk with them and try to learn from them. If I become lost and you come calling on me with disrespect, you will be put on indefinite hold! Our soul inspires us and can fulfill us in unimaginable ways, so let yours be one that will immortalize you.

THE AFTERLIFE?

WHILE IT WILL never be easy to say good-bye to someone that is close to us and we love so very much, we can take comfort in knowing that our good-byes are only temporary. I know we can no longer physically see them, hold them close to us, kiss their warm and gentle foreheads, or share our daily adventures with them. But we can take comfort in knowing that we will all be together once again somewhere in the afterlife. The notion that there exists an afterlife is a widely held belief that predates recorded history. More recent ideas suggest that life might continue in another dimension or plane of existence. Whatever the ideas, it's clear that we want to believe and perhaps even need to believe in life after death. There is no definitive proof, of course, that a life after death exists. And I know science suggests that these experiences are nothing more than the result of certain brain activity under extreme stress, but I believe these accounts should not be so easily dismissed. If they are real, after all, they hold the only clues we have as to what life in the hereafter might be like. As paranormal researchers, I believe that what we do is valuable and important as we strive to find any answers and proof that there may still be a presence of souls lost among us. For those lost souls, we reach out to you with open minds, open arms, and open hearts. Many may have moved on to their final destination, and I know it seems like everything shared between you and those you have lost becomes frozen in time for a moment, but take solace in the thought and the belief that you will be reunited one day with your loved ones. Hold their love everlasting within yourself and let it warm your very soul!

YOUR INTENDED AUDIENCE

A S PARANORMAL RESEARCHERS, we must try to understand our intended audience during an investigation. Of course, we may never know without any doubt that what is left here in our world is demonic in nature only, but my belief is that there are kind and gentle souls that are lost and searching that may remain among us. How we conduct ourselves will determine who our intended audience will be. As an investigator, if you don't feel love and compassion, then you don't feel sorrow, and not feeling this and giving the respect that accompanies it will bring you nothing good. We can't ever truly know what these lost and wandering souls went through, and we can't ever understand the depths of their pain and suffering in life. All we can do is listen as they try to convey their story to us. While we set up our equipment and the darkness of the night approaches, we need to keep in mind that what is here was once human like us. We must also be aware that what may be here could very well be demonic in nature and toy with our emotions to lead us to the dark side it dwells in. I believe a soul will retain memory and emotion as it did in the physical world. During life, if you loved and cared deep from your soul, then this would remain with the soul everlasting. So when I set out to find answers in the spiritual realm, I will begin my performance for my intended audience with respect, care, sorrow, and compassion. As I have said in the past, if I become one of these lost souls and you approach me with provocation, I will feel sorrow for you, and you will not like the response you receive. So please consider your intended audience before your performance in the night.

WE ARE A LOT ALIKE, YOU AND I

B OTH LOST SOULS and we are searching for the same thing. The realm of the paranormal and spirit world is wondrous and mysterious. We view it with wonder and awe; we become aware that this world is filled with spiritual life far beyond our comprehension. All of us play a part in understanding this realm, but none of us will ever have all the answers. When we enter into this realm that exists in the darkness and into our own hearts, we see that which we do not understand. We know that we have only touched on the surface of the unknown and yearn to learn more. We know that once we lose our soul, there is no turning back to what we once had. Everything we once dreamed of no longer exists, and we become lost and absent of answers. As we look to those that have moved to this unknown realm, we may pass in the darkness of night, not knowing that each of us is searching for the very same answers. Why do you remain? What exists beyond? What is next? Why? Other than our physical shell, we are so much the same as we are both lost and searching for answers. You, my lost and wandering friend, will know sooner than I of what exists beyond where I stand now. Thus, when I ask you for an answer, please respond so that I may gain insight to this wondrous and dark realm. Because we are a lot alike, you and I.

TALES FROM A GHOST TOWN

I REALLY LOVE writing about old ghost towns because of the many I have visited during my travels and the memories that unfold before me, both mine and the memories within their own mysterious and hypnotizing beauty! I stare in awe at the horizon that has been artistically painted and laid out before me, listening to its echoes from the distance as it recites its haunting story. The rolling and billowing clouds against the calming sky loom above the burning landscape below, which brings a solemn peacefulness to me. And on occasion, the sight of a drifting sagebrush as it dances through these now-dust-covered streets. Everything is still and silent, but you can sense the musical melody of life that once filled this desolate and wondrous place. A fluttering torn piece of cloth, once a curtain, blows through a broken and time-worn window, as if inviting me to walk inside and become a part of its lonesome atmosphere. Standing in haunting silence, I begin to hear the old wooden walkways begin to creak as if the souls, now passed, still venture through, searching for something absent of their being now. As I enter one of these beautiful monuments to history, I see a now-shattered mirror from which a reflection of times past still call out and beckon to me to share its memories. Though I may not see them there, the spirits see me. They watch me, and at times, they will reach out to me and begin to tell their stories. I find the beauty of these majestic and historical towns both mesmerizing and haunting. There is so much to learn from them, so when I visit these ghost towns, I do so with the respect and a true and passionate admiration! So tales of woe, tales of life, tales of happiness, tales of sorrow; I am always listening for tales from a ghost town!

TEARS FROM AN ANGEL

D O YOU BELIEVE in angels? I know that I do and always will. Angels in a variety of religions are regarded as spiritual beings. They are often depicted as messengers of God. The term "angel" has also been expanded to various notions of spiritual beings found in many other religious traditions. Other roles of angels include protecting and guiding human beings and carrying out divine tasks. In today's world, full of darkness, evil, and suffering, I think that we all need a bit of hope to hold on to. Angels possess infinite wisdom and spread their angelic melody across the earth and beyond. I believe that angels watch over us, and as they see and feel the suffering in the world, they shed delicate tears of sorrow for us. I believe there are times when our own personal angels will walk beside us in our times of need and share the tears that are wept by us. The tears of an angel are enchanting and gathered from deep in their very own souls. To be able to understand the world through the eyes of an angel would be profound beyond all expectations. Tears from an angel are cried for us, and their love and protection in dark times are often not seen or recognized by most in today's society. Most of us can actually feel our own guardian angels as they stand vigil over us when we need it the most, watching and shedding their warm and loving light with us. Much like when the clouds arrive and the storm is unleashed, only the flowers know the gift received after it subsides. The rose seems to know that life was shared as its petals glisten and its roots are once again refreshed in the cool autumn air by heaven's tears. We too can feel this when our angels cry for us as they share their heavenly melodies. Today's world can be hard and cruel. Stand up to it and stay strong! The song of life may fade for us one day but will live on through our souls. So when you are feeling down and need it, don't be afraid to cry and share your tears with the tears of your angel.

Team / Family / Unity

NOT ONLY SHOULD we seek unity in the paranormal community, but we also need to succeed in establishing unity within our own team dynamics. A paranormal group should consist of members with diverse beliefs and opinions to be cohesive and remain strong, standing as one! And those beliefs need to be respected and embraced by all members. No one member should stand above the others. This quote comes to mind: "The great leaders are like the best conductors—they reach beyond the notes to reach the magic in the players." This is so true in what we try to achieve as paranormal groups. People in every facet of life talk about building the team, working as a team, and my team, but few understand how to create the experience of teamwork or how to develop an effective team. Belonging to a team, in the broadest sense, is a result of feeling part of something larger than yourself. A strong team is one that sustains its members, respects them, supports and nourishes the members throughout, no matter the situation. All members must feel a freedom to express themselves freely within the group. As I visit some group pages out there, I see an arrogance about some in which team leaders and other members will belittle others in the group with "I'm right, you're not" attitudes. It's sad to see this among our teams today. Each and every member of a team is a valuable asset; their different beliefs should become part of the formula we need to succeed. Team of one, I think not! I have embraced all aspects within my team. We are family; we stand as one in unity and face all adversity that may come our way. Embrace your team's differences and work as one. Respect one another and unite in your effort, purpose, and cause. If this bothers you, maybe you are in the wrong place for all the wrong reasons!

SENSE THE DARKNESS

MOST PEOPLE RELATE sadness with darkness in almost every situation, both in the past and in today's world. Since ancient times, people have worn the color black to express their grief and sadness as if surrendering a part of life they were once warmly and affectionately attached to. Depression is almost always connected to darkness. Typically, you will read poems about darkness that automatically relate it to evil, sadness, and loss. Humanity has always feared the dark and what may exist within as it seems to lurk deep in the shadows and beckons us to join it. Although it may seem that darkness craves to devour the light we live in and those that exist around it, I embrace it! I feel there is a certain calming and tempting romance that lives in the darkness, something mysterious about it, which is hidden and unknown. There is a calm and serenity that I feel, a hypnotic silence I can hear, and peacefulness and emotion that only the darkness and I can share. I sit and listen to it and wait for its story to materialize before me. The darkness and the silence within it cause me to reflect. It stimulates my senses and allows me to see and feel the life that once existed within its cold and tightening grasp and exists there to this day. So when I stop and visit within this tranquil and unrelenting darkness, I begin to see more than I did when I walk in the light. Most may feel that this unrelenting darkness is much like an ongoing prayer that will never be answered, but I beg to differ. It is only in the soul-wrenching pitch-black darkness of the night that I really and truly begin to see! Can you sense the darkness?

A WHISPER IN THE NIGHT

I AM SURE this has happened to most of us. You lie there quietly in your bed enjoying your peaceful and well-deserved slumber when suddenly you are awakened by what you believe to be the voice of someone whispering and communicating with you. I have experienced this many times, and I disregard it as something I must have been dreaming of or must have heard in a confused state. Sometimes, the messages are crystal clear; sometimes, I cannot remember them or make any sense of them. Still, the question remains: Is there something from the spiritual realm trying to make contact with me? Is there a message some lost soul is trying to communicate to me? And if so, why do you believe they attempt this while we are in a dream state? We may be more vulnerable during this state and more apt to receive their message. There are many beliefs and many opinions on this subject. Why was it that I was chosen to receive this whisper in the night? It is my belief that there are those that wish to pass on a message to their loved ones that they did not have the chance to while they were here among us. This could be because they were taken before their time or because they never really had the chance or took the chance to give this gift of message to us. Yes, it could be just a dream, but in many cases, I believe there are loving and caring souls that want us to know that everything is okay or are passing on a message to us that could be warning us of impending doom. This has happened to me, and I have learned from it. If you ever have an experience with this phenomenon, please stop and listen for a message. There have been many life-changing experiences thanks to a whisper in the night!

LOST SOULS, WHO ARE THEY REALLY?

I HAVE CONTEMPLATED this for quite some time. "Lost souls," a sad term, yes. But as I stand alone in the vast and unrelenting darkness of any building during one of our paranormal investigations, searching for these poor, lost, and wandering spirits, waiting to hear their cries of terror or torment, I see the shadows that surround me and begin to wonder. Can these dark and ominous shadows in the calming silence turn against me? I do not mean physically but in a mental and emotional capacity. What dark secrets live in these still walls? What stories can they tell me? They cause me to reflect on myself and where my life is right now as I try and make sense of all that happens around me. I think to myself, Why am I here? What is my final goal in this life? What if . . . ? I find no answer that can satisfy me, so I ask you, who really is the lost soul here? The spirit that dwells here, lives in its walls, quietly whispers in its darkness, knows the echoing and dark secrets that are hidden within. I do not, so I ask again, who is the lost soul here? Are the screams that I hear in the distance from something that exists in the shadows and searches for a reply and the companionship that once warmed its soul? Or is it my own soul screaming out as I walk along the edge of sanity and stray just steps away from my own demons that await for that one missed step that will cause me to stray and fall so that they may devour me and my soul? We are all here to learn something, something of a profound nature, something to take us forward on this journey, where the shadows can turn against us. Stay strong, stay focused in life, live, and love while you still can. Come to terms with where you are now so you do not end up a lost soul.

CONTACT FROM ABOVE

I HEAR THIS constantly: "I was visited last night by someone I cared about long ago and has since passed." There exists much religious skepticism on this matter as most of them will tell you that once someone has passed, their soul goes either directly to heaven or to hell, never to make contact again, and all that remains can only be determined to be demonic in nature. I beg to differ here, and I feel strongly about this! It is my belief that the love once shared between those that have since passed is a love that extends deep into our souls; thus, it exists in the soul and spirit once it moves on. To have once felt someone lying in your arms as they slowly drift off to sleep and you stare in contentment at how gentle and beautiful they are, the soft, warm hugs and gentle kisses, the sharing of emotions, both good and bad. To feel the warmth and love of their hearts, to share that laughter and the sorrowful tears that only those and yourself could have felt in your very own ways, to live in warmth of the bond and love that was created by you and the angels that have passed on. These are all things that we as humans nurture and grow between one another and, in my opinion, are everlasting. Good souls do remain behind, and if they do move on, they watch over us from heaven. I do not care how clever and misleading an evil spirit may be; there is no possible way that it could duplicate or even imitate that deep loving and emotional state that has been created by you and your angel. So if you are touched by your angel and it uplifts your soul, keep the belief alive. Love is from our heart and soul. Let it warm your heart and live within you as you dwell in its light until the day we are all reunited with our special angels! *Contact from above?* I definitely say yes and will hold it true until my last breath is taken from me in this world!

Thou Shalt Not Fear

MARK TWAIN ONCE said, "Courage is resistance to fear, mastery of fear—not absence of fear."

Mr. Twain hits the nail right on the head every time! I know I won't lie, and to be perfectly honest, I could crap my pants from the fear I encounter in some of the areas that I crawl into as a paranormal investigator! But if you show courage and resist the fear, stay, and face it, you, my friend, have then mastered it! Never be ashamed of feeling fear. There should never be an absence of fear in what we do whether in everyday life or in the paranormal field. It's quite normal and healthy and aids in our growth. When someone says, "I have no fear of anything," I have to raise the BS flag on that one. All of us feel fear in some form; there is absolutely no way around it. What differentiates us from others is how we deal with it. So feel the fear, live with the fear, face the fear, and never let it define who you are as an individual! Fear, you are my friend and a driving force in what I do. I will always hold you as a close companion! I will embrace fear and learn from it as it teaches me to become stronger. There will never be a time when I will try to hide my fear because, in the end, it's what will define me!

PARANORMAL EXISTENCE

It is wonderful that five thousand years have now elapsed since the creation of the world, and still it is undecided whether or not there has ever been an instance of the spirit of any person appearing after death. All argument is against it; but all belief is for it.

—Samuel Johnson

I HAVE TO admit, the argument against paranormal existence is sometimes overwhelming. But as Samuel Johnson states, all belief is for it. We as paranormal investigators carry on that belief; we embrace it, and we use it as our driving force to discovery! You cannot argue all the bits and pieces of substantial evidence captured by paranormal groups. Sure, there are those who will present so-called evidence, faked or doctored to make it seem more than it really is, and sensationalize the entire process and experience. But we, as dedicated researchers, must stay on the path to legitimate evidence and present it in a true and professional manner for others to try and understand. Listen, even though others are out there doing what we do for the wrong reasons, stay true to your beliefs. Do not be discouraged, and keep striving forward. The path that leads us to answers is a difficult one, riddled with obstacles and unanswered questions. But if we had all the answers, it wouldn't be called research, would it! Keep striving for the answers and stick to your belief in paranormal existence. This is our cause!

ARE WE CASUALTIES OF WAR BETWEEN GOOD AND EVIL?

I S IT OUR personal religious beliefs and practices that make us more or less vulnerable to spiritual attack and attachments during our paranormal research? I believe this to be so. I consider myself to be a religious and spiritual being. However, I am not as good at heart as some, so does this make me more or less vulnerable during an investigation for a malevolent entity to wage its attack? If an encounter is made with a dark and malicious force, it is my belief that it will target someone that is more pure at heart and try to lead them, by deceit, to the dark realm that they inhabit and grow stagnant in. We have to know and remember that anything demonic in nature is intelligent and will try to bring us down with them. Listen, the battle between good and evil has already been fought, way before any of us ever existed, and evil lost! All the dark realm can do now is try to bring what is still good and living in the light down into the empty and tormenting darkness with it. So protect yourself and prepare for your own personal war with evil. Stay true to your faith and do not become one of these casualties of war!

PREPARE FOR BATTLE!

THERE IS A spiritual battle we face on a day-to-day basis between good and evil. What is it exactly? Do we notice it? Do we just ignore it? In my opinion, we see it in everything, and we see it in all people. We all possess the ability to create evil, but most choose not to. Spiritual evil does exist. It is my belief that the powers of darkness have learned well to disguise themselves. As I have mentioned prior, malevolent spirits can appear to us as anything of their choosing. We are an easy and captive audience to their production and manipulation. In the beginning, evil had already lost the battle and is now attempting to take as many lost souls down with it. Evil searches out a weakness, then attaches itself to it and feeds from it. We do not know exactly what it attaches to or how it pulls off this dark and deviate process. This battle rages each and every second of each and every day. Just because we can't see it doesn't mean it does not exist! Believe me when I say that we do not deal with this solely in paranormal research. This is present within all of us, present all around us, and it has existed longer than any of us. As long as we choose the good, we will have conquered and won our personal war, but the battle will wage on until the end of time. Always remain prepared for battle!

POPULARITY CONTEST

I HAVE BEEN visiting a lot of paranormal sites and pages recently and noticed many comments about their fear that people's interest in the paranormal is starting to fade. This bugs me in a major way, and let me tell you why. We as paranormal research groups are not here to become famous or to win any sort of popularity contest. Whether others are losing interest in the paranormal has absolutely nothing to do with us and what we should or do stand for. We are here solely to study and try to understand the spiritual realm and attempt to share answers with those who are also trying to understand. If we are true to our beliefs and dedicated to this field, popularity should not matter. Research, study, respect, learning, and answers should be our only concerns. Along with this, we need to add sharing valid and legitimate points with others. If we truly possess the passion for the paranormal and believe in finding the answers for the right reasons, then winning a popularity contest should never be an issue. Being better than others should never be an issue. Being part of some elite and wondrous group should not be an issue. What should be the issue is our passion for the paranormal and what exists within its grasp. That is just my belief, and I would hope that most of you share in this attitude and belief!

I Wonder

A S I WALK through this cold, dark, silent, and abandoned building that once was warm and full of life, I wonder, here in the stillness and silence, what it must have been like in times past. Was there happiness? Was there sadness? Did anger exist here? Did remnants of love echo through its hallways? Or was it always cold, dark, and eloquently empty like this? I hear a noise in the distance, then a whispering breath, as if someone is trying to say something. I wonder who this might be. I wonder, why have you chosen me to communicate to and not others who have trod through your dark and ominous passages before me? I wonder, are you a kind spirit that has lost your way in the night or a prowling creature living in the shadows, waiting to draw me into the darkness and devour my light and soul also? I wonder as I continue to walk through the blinding and cruel blackness, are you lonely? Do you want to be remembered? Do you feel as I do now? Do you miss the physical touch of others that once warmed you and cared for you? I wonder, after the flame of life was taken from you and its lingering smoke faded into the blackness and emptiness of this place, why does your soul remain? I am not arrogant enough to think that I have found you. I know that it is you that has chosen me to come forward and share your solemn message. But the reason escapes me as I stand in the growing bleakness and denseness of this place, so I wonder!

LISTEN TO THEM

WHEN I FIRST walk into a historic and majestic building, I listen to the silence. I hear the silence. I see and I feel the dark and enlightening shadows that linger within its tranquil and illusive walls. Every building has its own story to tell, and if you listen closely, you will hear it speak to you as it unfolds before you, almost as if it is singing a song of what once was, a melodious tune that wants you to hear its symphony. All you need to do is open your eyes, your ears, and your mind to see and hear the wondrous performance and to feel its angelic tune that has been orchestrated for you and others throughout time. The image of a lone child's shoe lying on the floor, which once encased a little one's foot as they ran and played without a care in the world, an abandoned bed once slumbered in by someone who shared their feelings and passions of life, and a dark and broken chair missing the companionship of warm human contact. These remnants in time all have a story to tell. It was alive and vibrant here once. People walked through its corridors. They laughed, they cried, they all shared stories as they wandered through these dark and hypnotic passages. Now these buildings sit alone and abandoned with only memories of a life long past. When you visit these wonderful and beautiful monuments to time, respect them, explore them, and listen to the magnificent stories they have to tell. Alone in their sadness, let them share with you the tales of a life it was once host to. The souls of these spectacular structures are reaching out to us and want us to listen to their stories! Let's all open our minds, our eyes, our ears, and our emotions and listen to what they have to share with us! Respect them, share with them, and most importantly, listen to them!

148

BECAUSE I ALREADY KNOW

IS THERE ANOTHER realm that exists beyond our physical world? My answer is yes. I can honestly say this because I have seen the apparition of a woman walking the halls of a cold and abandoned hospital, generating her own light source. I have seen the materialization of a small child as she appeared next to me during the night wearing a hospital robe, arms hanging straight down as she stood and stared right through me, as if sharing her misery and loneliness. I have heard voices calling out in the darkness, trying to pass on some sort of devastating message or maybe even beckoning me to come closer to where they exist and share some light in the cold and overwhelming shadows that have taken over their being. I have felt the anger, the sadness, and the emptiness that linger in that dark and black place and, on occasion, the physical touch of another, as if reaching out to a world that they once were part of and miss so much. Some might just dismiss these experiences as anomalous or not meaningful or even to their imagination. Or out of fear or personal beliefs, some may not be ready to know that there is another realm, full of unknowns and occupied by darkness and uncertainty. By all means, I am not here to force my beliefs on anyone. All I can do is share my experiences and let others form their own opinions, which I respect in every way! So the path that I so passionately follow now is to find the answers that others fear! I need not prove to myself, nor do I look to others to accept my word as proof, because I already know!

IF IT WERE ME

YES, I DO think about it! If I were to become one of the poor, lost, and wandering souls we so desperately search out in the night, will I still feel as I tread through the cold blinding and empty darkness? Being free of the physical shell I once inhabited, will I still miss the things I enjoyed in life? I believe that if we will still indeed feel after departing this world, I will miss the soft and tender touch of my loving wife and her kind, warm, and caring heart. I will miss seeing a single flower growing from the ground as I walk through my warm and sunlit yard. I will miss the smiles and the laughter once shared with me by those I loved and cared for so very much. I will miss watching a lone snowflake falling to the ground or getting caught in the rain as it soaked me through and through. I will miss the fun times, the laughter, the tears, the hard times, and those that I loved and experienced these emotions with. I will miss feeling my bare feet walking through the soft green grass or kicking up the sand on an ocean-sprayed beach as I watch the clouds begin to gather above, adding to its picturesque beauty. I will miss all these things and more. But I will also know that even though I am alone and cold in the dark, I will be remembered and be in the thoughts of those I cared about and those that cared about me, which will bring about a warmth that soothes me. I don't want to miss these things once I pass on but will be grateful for it as it will mean I enjoyed it during my life! That is my take . . . if it were me!

FINDING ANSWERS, OTHERS FEAR

"RESEARCH," JUST ANOTHER word for gathering information. But why do we do it? As we state in our logo with the Paranormal Research Group of Utah, to "find answers that others fear." In today's world, there are more and more people each day that encounter the paranormal in some way or another and are looking for some explanation, some answers. With paranormal research, many people are too hasty to make decisions without gathering the information and proof first. Research requires time, effort, and dedication. It is the basis to what we try to do as researchers. We as investigators have to remain focused and open-minded in our research. We still know so little about this realm. There is a frontier (paranormal research), which requires our journey and exploration to face the unknowns. It impacts many now and in the future. There are consequences for presenting evidence you believe is paranormal in nature or of the spirit world before you have studied it thoroughly. This can be detrimental to our cause. People that follow and trust us can lose interest, and before you know it, we lose our legitimacy as professional researchers and paranormal groups. There are those out there in the paranormal world that just become frustrated and call it quits after years of not capturing any hard evidence of spiritual existence. Listen, even Thomas Edison encountered many failures before inventing the first practical electric lightbulb in 1879. Nobody saw the years of effort and the number of failures he had to face for that single life-defining moment. Don't let your unsuccessful pursuits dishearten you. Let sheer indulgence reinstate the belief that you will see light at the end of the tunnel. I am in this for the long haul. I will learn from my mistakes. I will remain focused, and I will always share my findings and ask for your help in determining its true meaning! Remain true to your beliefs and stay the path! Our research is vital; it guards us against misinformation, it provides guidance for others to base a decision on, and it helps build that road that leads others to an understanding and eventually gains the respect for those involved and guides us to that final destination, finding answers, others fear!

'TIS NOT THE NUMBERS THAT DEFINE YE

THERE WAS ONCE upon a time a certain people who had set forth on a journey, a journey for knowledge and kinship among its members. Many lands then existed where they could gather as one. But alas, their hopes were stricken and dreams of such a wonderful place shattered before them as they would soon realize a darkness lying in wait. As they traveled near and far, they came upon a place where there reigned a king, one who promised them many things, and such a braggart was this person as he boasted of the masses in number that occupied his lands. "Gaze upon what I have created and feel free to join us here as I shall add you to our great and powerful numbers!" said this king. These people, their dreams and hopes reborn, joined the masses and began to share henceforth their beliefs and values within this realm. These kind and weary travelers found themselves among a strange people who thusly attacked their beliefs and were full of ridicule and deceit. "How is it that a place of so many in number can show such an unkindness and disconcertment?" asked the people. The self-announced king thus ordered it to be proclaimed throughout the whole of his kingdom that whosoever shall defy him shall be banned from interaction with the masses yet still tallied within its numbers. Most dared not oppose this dark and false king for fear of the terrors that might follow such an act. But these were not an ignorant people. They gathered in field and in forest with spirits full of sorrow and sadness. "Dare we venture on? For we are such a small number," asked they to one another. Determined and resilient was the decision rendered that they must continue their trek. Not far from this terrible place was a chasm that led to another land. The good people followed this path and stumbled into a place filled with light and populated by those who shared the same hope, the same dream. They wondered how such a place, wonderful as it might be, could survive with a population so small in number. Those that dwelled within said unto the weary travelers, "'Tis not the number that matters in what we do but the knowledge which is amassed that gives us strength and power like no other!" They then rejoiced and found comfort in the thought that they had found a home, a place free of ridicule and doubt, a place where diverse beliefs, opinions, and values were shared, and a knowledge grew within them. These people had found a home. These people had found a *family*! Hence, from this day forward, they stood as one and learned happily ever after.

LET NOT ARROGANCE DEFINE YE

ONCE UPON A time, in the Realm of Paranormal Family, there lived an arrogant people who thusly feasted upon the hope and aspirations of the townspeople who had gathered within and now dwelled there. They were heard talking to one another of the strength and of the resilience possessed by this Paranormal Family, who now inhabited this wonderful and mysterious place. Those arrogant were in fear of how no one among them could break the bond now formed within this strong and diverse clan. The naysayers decided among them that they shall belittle and instill a dark and evil doubt unto this Paranormal Family. So on the morrow, they unleashed their ill-gotten plan and blew in a storm of ridicule not seen by any man to this very day!

"Oh the arrogance," responded those within the family. "Such a pity that we doest not defend thyself with harsh and loaded words in response," thought the well-rooted and diverse people.

"'Tis better we do not sink to a level inhabited by only the ignorant from which no return is possible," stated the family. Hence, that very day the family stood against this adversary and did not let their ramblings deter their very being from achieving that in which they so desperately held in hope. This evil foe had never conceivably imagined the strength within the family as they stood as one. "Let it be known throughout the lands that we stand together, we stand proud, and we stand united. Let no person come between us, for they shall feel the wrath of the valiant blade of our bond and fall in devastating defeat. Hence, from this very day, I decree there is peace and belonging once again within the Paranormal Family." And so they learned happily ever after!

LET'S MAKE THE DIFFERENCE

HAVE YOU EVER wondered why, a lot of times, you just can't seem to make any progress in what you endeavor to achieve as a paranormal investigator? There just seems to be a void that lies between what you know and what you actually are able to prove. There are those out there who will succumb to their frustration and just give up on their visions and hopes to find the answers we seek out as paranormal researchers. Don't let this happen to you! Though we have only but scratched the surface in our understanding, we will eventually succeed in spite of the extreme difficulties we will face. It is your mind-set that will determine whether or not you have what it takes to continue the journey we face together. There lives a certain strength and fire within us, a very unique and positive power that can lift and carry us forward, no matter the obstacles before us. If we are to ever find answers and gain knowledge and understanding of a long-hidden realm, we must have the mind-set to continue in the face of all adversity without fail! If there is any hope at all out there to find and add reason to these haunting occurrences, it is us that will bring it to the light. It is through our determination and constant trek forward that a path can be laid for all to follow, both now and in the future. To those who give up and to those who will speak out against us, I say, so freaking what! We are not here purely for their entertainment; we are not here to sell ourselves, and we do not exist for their pleasure. Hell, the truth is, we have nothing to sell! We need only believe in ourselves and in the visions we have set. Our drive and our passion shall define us. So with our true aspiration to succeed, we can arouse feelings within us that will rekindle hope, strengthen our faith, and empower our determination and motivation toward reaching our goals. Trust in yourself. Believe in your teams, and together, we will make the difference!

CHOOSE MEMORIES OVER LONELINESS

YOU KNOW, I write a lot about the paranormal and all the things we deal with as researchers in this field. There are so many emotions out there from a lot of my friends just from the discussions we share together, and the subject of loneliness after losing a loved one comes up often. So for now, let's just focus on this and nothing else. Loneliness sometimes can seem very overwhelming when you are missing a loved one that has since passed. A little loneliness can be healthy in ways at times, but to dwell in it for extended periods of time will draw you into the darkness as a permanent fixture in the shadows, causing you to abandon everyone and everything that you once held dear. You can light a path and find your way out, escape by one simple little thing we all call memories. Remember all the things that you shared with your loved ones when you were together and stop focusing on the pain! Your memory will connect you once again with those you loved as you share your warm thoughts between you and them. Remember the times you had together, the jokes you shared, and the laughter that filled the room. Remember those times you walked together, staring at the blue heavens above you as you held each other's hand and knew that nothing could ever take this feeling away. Remember the peaceful serenity shared between you and how it felt just right. Remember how perfect it was being with each other as your love grew from day to day. Even the memories of sad times, sorrow, and pain should lift you as you know you shared them together and became stronger from them. Let the loneliness go, release it like dust into a gentle breeze of memory, and let it float away as the memories' breeze blows fresh upon your face and cleanses you. Those that have passed would not want to see you lonely and withering away. They would want you to keep those memories alive, for they know that one day, you will both share them together once again. As long as their memory remains within you, the loneliness you feel will fade. The memories of a loved one will never be erased from our minds. They are meant to be remembered and cherished for life eternal. So I ask you for this one favor: choose your memories over the loneliness!

OUR PASSION, OUR PATH

RECENTLY, I TOOK some time off and visited some different places out there, meeting many interesting individuals along the way. I came to the realization that others share in the passion that we all have in our dealings with the paranormal in general. Whether they were part of a paranormal group or just shared in the interests and the haunting mystery of the subject itself, I found a true and motivating passion that lifted my own even more. Our passion in what we do is a wonderful gift of our spirit combined with all the experiences we have collected over our lifetime. It endows each and every one of us with the power to strive forward and continue our journey with unbridled enthusiasm! When we use our minds, bodies, and spirits as one to focus on our individual beliefs, we remain true to our beliefs and then become an unwavering force. Our passion enables us to overcome the obstacles and adversities that we will encounter along the way. The possibilities and potential that exist within us are infinite, and when we choose our passion to reinforce our beliefs, we are able to progress by leaps and bounds. So by no means should you let anyone tell you different and stray you from your path! There are those that will attempt to bring you down. Stay focused and you will sense the lying wolf waiting to pounce and feed off you and your positive attitude, wanting to devour your visions and dreams. In their lack of sincerity and passion, they will try to lure you to their level. Stay true to your passion and believe in yourself, and these impostors will soon fade away as nothing but a bitter memory! Many of the limitations we face in life are self-imposed, and how we view them and choose to deal with them will determine our outcome. I choose to remain passionate; I choose to stay the path. There are many out there who think and believe as we do. They share the passion, they have the determination, they possess the desire and respect, and this, in itself, lifts me up and keeps me striving forward! Keep your passion alive and stay the path!

OH, MIGHTY DIVERSITY

ONCE UPON A time in a land filled with countless paranormal research teams, there existed a team that stood as one, a strong and resilient force in the realm. How did this come to pass? you may ask yourself. This small group of curious and dedicated people had gathered together from different lands and proclaimed to one another that they shall undertake a journey such as no other in the realm had ever dreamed to endeavor. Based on their very differences, they would strike out on a journey, a trek that would bring them ever closer together and create a bond that no mortal man could ever attempt to undo. There were many others that would dare this endeavor, and though some would achieve it, there were many that would fail. As they were not successful in their undertaking of Team Unity and betrayal had reared its ugly head and became their closest companion, all loyalties and strengths were thusly forfeited, and it came to pass that they would stand alone as they awaited the misfortunes that would soon befall them. Those within the realm that would embrace these diversities that were now a part of each would resolve them to stand in awe and speak not, but instead gaze in astonishing wonderment at the mysteries and wonders as they would begin to unfold before their very eyes. Thereupon, the group proclaimed that in their respect for one another and in their combined passion, they would stand against all adversity and follow their path to the journey's end. You know, I don't get it, but writing in this format tends to catch the interest of most out there. I say it a lot and will always stand for diversity among team members and the acceptance of each and every belief no matter how much we differ from one another. Those who do not do this and want everyone to be the same or else are doing nothing but hurting themselves and what they are working together to accomplish. So I end with this final statement: Let it be said and stated as such upon this very day that we are as one and will make this wondrous journey together. Let no obstacle deter us from that which we so desperately and passionately seek. Let us learn and gain the knowledge as one and stand as an unwavering force in the tormenting winds of adversity. I stand in awe and I stand proud with my team and all that they have accomplished! So it is said, so it is done.

LET HE WHO IS WITH ALL KNOWLEDGE CAST THE FIRST STONE!

I SEE THIS quite a bit on our pages here in the Paranormal Community. Someone may believe that they have an EVP or what they think may be a picture or video of a valid capture of something paranormal in nature. Then like a baited hook dropped into the shark-infested waters of doubt, their post is attacked, mutilated, and eaten alive by those who believe that they know all there is to know about everything. These self-proclaimed experts in this field are just that, in my opinion—self-proclaimed! Listen, I know that there are those out there who really do care and really do want to help another out when it comes to analyzing evidence, but I have also come to realize that some are arrogant enough to come off as all-knowing. None of us have all the answers in what we seek in this realm. I will be first to admit that I learn something new each and every day. But there will never be a day that even I could be an expert. It has gotten to the point where investigators are reluctant in their posting of evidence for fear of ridicule and aggressive attacks from these stone-casting, arrogant beings. This is just something we must deal with on a daily basis in what we do and are trying to achieve. I can take respectful and genuine criticism, and I will learn from it as we all should. But when arrogance enters the arena and these confrontational beings enter to feed and swell their egos even more, my weapon of preference is a laugh mixed with pity and a touch of the Delete button. So post everything you may think is something! The worse that can happen is you can learn from the people that do it for the right reasons and in a respectful way. As for the stone-throwers, just feel sorry for them, wipe them from your shoes, and continue your journey!

Just For Laughs
The National Paragraphic
Society Presents . . .

AHHHH, THE EVER-SO-ILLUSIVE paranormal investigator. In this rare camera footage, we were able to capture a glimpse of them in their natural habitat. Notice how they sit/stand in wait as they prepare for the night's hunt. Their insatiable appetite for knowledge and answers has driven them to adapt to their surroundings as they stalk their unsuspecting prey. Or is it the other way around? We may never know! We were very lucky to catch this photo. As you can see, another member of the pride stands and watches as the alpha male prepares for the hunt. Though much of the time the pride hunts as a group, it has been known that eventually they will separate into individual cliques to cover more territory as they stalk their prey, hiding in the shadows. They basically hunt at night as they move slowly and meticulously through the darkness in search of answers. The clan will then hibernate during the following day of their investigation and, after awakening, will feed on their captures as they proceed to the evidence review. Generally, the alpha male feeds first and, when satisfied, shares with others within the pride. This day, he has fed well and proceeds to initiate a never-before-seen ritualistic dance in celebration of evidence of his captured prey. Is this a dance of victory? Is it the dance of pride or maybe some sort of mating ritual? We may never know. But one thing is for sure; it kind of looks stupid! So as we move on and leave this wondrous and elusive pride to its mysterious ways, we can take comfort in knowing that the paranormal investigator is strong and determined in its endeavor for survival. So beware and stand vigil in the night for that is when they leave their dens to satisfy their insatiable appetite for knowledge. And if you look and listen closely in the silence of night, there is a good chance that even you will catch a rare glimpse of these creatures as you hear their haunting howls of "WTF was that?"

JUST SAYIN'!

NOW IS THE time that those of us in the paranormal community need to unite because it is us who are genuinely insisting on real answers to real questions! It is also the time that the media, specifically television shows about the paranormal, serve the public more diligently than they do their own ratings or advertisers. Some of the individuals who appear on these shows themselves should be the ones ashamed of claiming items as paranormal when it is obvious they are not. How about a show directly after with follow-up questions from other guests that don't buy the steaming pile of make-believe? Shouldn't we all be more interested in accomplishing something over being something? There is a great and differentiating aspect between being an individual who truly cares about the paranormal and being a celebrity. Basically, these televised regurgitations should have the surgeon general's warning pasted directly to the credits with the main point being this—may cause blind stupidity and ignorance! Listen, I know it's all for ratings, and I know the producers don't believe most of what some of these want-to-bes say or do. But at the same time, there are those of us dedicating ourselves fully for the right reasons, and I tend to find it a bit frustrating when I am queried about it from clients and others only due to the fact they have seen it on TV. Though I will always remain focused in my purpose, I will always hold a bit of putrid discernment toward those absent of any morals or standards. Just sayin'!

It's Sensational! . . . Ism

I N OUR CURRENT circumstances, our efforts as paranormal investigators are in danger of becoming a target of entrenched and oft-welcomed television sensationalism by the uninformed that choose to watch and believe for the sole reason of it being exciting and on television. This sensationalizing of the paranormal causes a trend in which people expect those of us who do it not for fame and fortune but for all the right reasons to look like boring amateurs. Thus, our legitimacy fades and set in anticipation of that haunting particle of dust or amazing camera glare that just leaves them in drooling awe. How do we as paranormal investigators defend against this onslaught of media sensationalism and protect what all that we attempt to achieve? The answer is quite simple; who gives a sh—! We know why we do it, and that in itself should suffice. I'm not here for fame or fortune; I am here to find out why these things occur in an unknown realm. I am not here to sugarcoat it, nor do I intend to get out my can of happy-ass rainbow and butterfly-colored paint and airbrush a fairy-tale masterpiece for the willing to revel in and pee all over themselves. This is not wonderland or the land of make-believe; what we do is real as we search for real answers to real questions. Sensationalism in today's society is not an issue in my book. That's my take!

LET'S ROLL THE DICE!

COMPARATIVELY SPEAKING, EACH time we conduct a paranormal investigation, it is much like rolling the dice. Let's say, for instance, that you hold a dice in your hand that contains a thousand sides to it and is numbered accordingly. As you roll the dice, trying to land on a specific number, it may take years before you hit that one number, but you will eventually hit it after determined and constant attempts. With this mind-set, we can look past the adversities of today, which we face on a constant in the paranormal field. The perennial conviction that those who work hard and devote themselves fully to the long haul will be rewarded in the end stands true in this case. We must continue to believe that tomorrow will be better than today as we continue to endeavor in our efforts to find proof and answers in a realm riddled with mystery. The rolling of this proverbial dice started in years long past and times long ago. It has been handed down through history and now lies in our hands as we remain determined to hit that one certain number—proof of the existence of another realm! None of us are perfect, nor are we perfectible, but with our resilience and dedication to a purpose, we can keep the dream alive as we continue on our journey. We have overcome so many challenges in this field and faced many obstacles. The allure of the belief that we possess the capacity to make a difference is what defines each of us and ignites that strength within. We become stronger each day as we gather even closer to rolling that number. And as our dreams and visions grow more powerful each day by the knowledge shared by others in our time, so does the possibilities of rolling that perfect number and finding the answers. So grasp that dice tightly, open your mind, keep your passion alive, and continue to roll today, tomorrow, and into the future. Our number is coming up!

Our spirit and passion for the paranormal does not by any ways or means emerge out of nowhere. It is formed and defined with time and by the people who have dedicated themselves to understanding it, embracing it, and sharing it with others. There is no doubt that those of us who have shared in this passion and hoped for answers in the past, now, and in the future will become an integral part of its legacy. As we take this paranormal passion and combine it with our own diverse beliefs and our individual approach to life and personalize it to the point of sharing and learning, we then begin to make a difference as we build a map for future investigators to follow. What makes up this spirit and passion, you may ask? I would venture to say that it is our ethics, compassion, creativity, beliefs, determination, and willingness to take risks that drive us forward. We hear plenty of talk out there about who is best in the field or who may be a true expert when in reality we know there is no basis that can measure this. Sure, there are those with considerably more experience, but even then, we still need to add that to the mix and continue to build and learn above and beyond what most settle for now. We see it on television, we read about it in articles, we hear about it on the radio from self-proclaimed experts, and it sometimes affects newer, less-experienced groups from jumping in and getting their feet wet. But when we stop and really look, we will see that the reality is, this field cannot be measured, quantified, or calculated to the point where we can determine one individual is better than another. It is our gathering of knowledge as we share between one another that our combined efforts will be the hope that our success is borne of. Learning together and gathering this information is what will establish the way forward. Let the only influences you face in this field be positive ones and not those of arrogance and negativity. Let your spirit and your passion for the paranormal endure!

As we all pause and begin to learn from our experiences in the paranormal, we become more committed in the effort to motivate, to inspire, and to both teach and learn from everything we encounter and share on a day-to-day basis. This enhances our ability to view our research from a diverse and much-broader perspective. Every bit of information shared becomes invaluable, condensed pieces of wisdom that enlighten the mind and awaken it to the truth and knowledge now concealed by something within the realm or by our very own closed-mindedness. We are all very much like beacons in the night that illuminate the passageway to knowledge, to inspiration, and to the answers in our search. We gather our strength from one another and, in the process, learn and grow! As we learn from one another in the present and use our experiences from the past, then and only then do we begin to build our future. Sometimes in able to discover what is true in the realm of the paranormal will demand freedom from tradition, which means freedom from all fears, whether it be the doubt, ridicule, or any adversity that will arise.

As you can see from these thoughts of mine, I have a deep and serious passion for the paranormal and a deep desire to learn what may exist in an afterlife. All that I have experienced throughout my journey through this unknown realm has played a major role in my life that has sharpened my senses and developed a new respect for all that exists within its shadowy and tightening grasp. When I walk in the footsteps of souls that have passed away, there is that moment when I am able to experience and even become a part of that perfect and harmonious symphony they have laid out before me. There is a mysterious and wondrous spectrum of color that they have painted in the blindness of the night that guides me and shares emotions they have felt as they once lived. Though frightened at times as I walk these dark passages, I can feel them walking side by side with me, as if sharing a casual stroll and wanting for that companionship they no longer have the ability to feel. I may not clearly see them as they accompany me on my journey, but I can feel them, I can hear their stories, I can feel their emotions, and I can finally sense the loneliness as it pierces my soul, for that is where they have become entrapped. As their shadows roam through these dark halls and pathways that are illuminated only by a light and teasing hints of moonlight, a story is being told. Please take the time to listen to these stories and respect what is being shared with you.

It has taken a lot for me to be able to shift from one state of consciousness to an entirely different state of reality. We are typically driven to certain realities by the various brain processes we utilize and our mind-sets in life. There will come a defining moment where you too may come face-to-face with one of these life-changing experiences that will affect your outlook and the way that you conduct yourself in your paranormal research. When I first began to follow my interests in the paranormal, I was one of those hotshots that just craved the thrill and would do anything for a response from a spirit without any care for who may be affected by my behavior. I was disrespectful and looking for just one thing and one thing only—the thrill. As I look back on how I behaved in the past, I feel sorry for myself and am thankful for the changes I have made. Don't get me wrong; to this very day, I still use provocation but only in cases dealing with malevolent haunting and only to a point. I now emulate a serious and genuine respect and utilize all measures of protecting myself and those around me.

When all is said and done, I guess the point that I want to make is this: the existence of a paranormal realm and activity within it is very real. It has always been there and always will. Proving it is a different subject altogether. It is how we go about it that will truly define us as human beings and add to our legitimacy in this field of study. Those of you who do it to be famous, those of you who do it for the bragging rights, and those of you who do it exclusively to get your own television series and add to the sensationalism, by all means, please continue. But stop for a moment and think about the right reasons we do what we do. Put yourselves in the shoes of those who have passed on and become part of a dark and unknown realm. Then ask yourself this one simple question: "Is this how I want to be seen and treated when I move on?" As I stated earlier, these spirits were once like us. They had loved ones, they lived, they laughed, they cried, they loved, and they felt as we do now. Do not belittle them or treat them as animals or creatures of the night. Treat them with respect and as human beings.

In closing, paranormal research and study are vital. We as paranormal groups should not be in competition with one another or embrace the belief that we are better in any form or matter. We are all here for the same reason, and by sharing our experiences with one another, we can strive forward together and as one insurmountable force. The paranormal and/or spiritual realm has existed for a millennium as has the evidence of its existence. It is up to us to search for the answers, but we have to do it in a respectful and meaningful manner. We need to document it, dissect it, and then present it as a valid and legitimate proof. My passion for the paranormal has been and always will be a driving force in my life! All I ask is that you come and share it with me as we all continue our journey to the answers others fear amid the shadows!

Thank you to Anna Price, Geoffrey Brown, Gordon Hughes, "Rocky," Marcy Casey, and Felicia McMichael—my team, my crew, and my family!

www.ingramcontent.com/pod-product-compliance
Lightning Source LLC
Chambersburg PA
CBHW022231290526
45785CB00014B/715